Founding Sisters
and the Nineteenth Amendment

Preeminent writers offering fresh, personal
perspectives on the defining events of our time

Published Titles

William Least Heat-Moon, *Columbus in the Americas*

Scott Simon, *Jackie Robinson and
the Integration of Baseball*

Alan Dershowitz, *America Declares Independence*

Thomas Fleming, *The Louisiana Purchase*

Forthcoming Titles

Douglas Brinkley on the March on Washington

William F. Buckley Jr. on the Fall of the Berlin Wall

Bob Edwards on Edward Murrow and
the Birth of Broadcast Journalism

Sir Martin Gilbert on D-Day

Martin Goldsmith on the Beatles Coming to America

Founding Sisters
and the Nineteenth Amendment

ELEANOR CLIFT

WILEY

John Wiley & Sons, Inc.

Published by John Wiley & Sons, Inc., Hoboken, New Jersey
Published simultaneously in Canada

Design and production by Navta Associates, Inc.

For general information about our other products and services, please contact our Customer Care Department within the United States at (800) 762-2974, outside the United States at (317) 572-3993 or fax (317) 572-4002.

Wiley also publishes its books in a variety of electronic formats. Some content that appears in print may not be available in electronic books. For more information about Wiley products, visit our web site www.wiley.com.

Library of Congress Cataloging-in-Publication Data:

Clift, Eleanor, date.
   Founding sisters and the Nineteenth Amendment / Eleanor Clift.
      p.   cm.
Includes bibliographical references.

   1. Women—Suffrage—United States—History. 2. Suffragists—United States—History. I. Title.
   JK1896.C55 2003
   324.6'23'092273—dc21

                                                                      2003011761

   ISBN 978-0-471-42612-7 (hc)
   ISBN 978-1-68442-227-2 (pbk.)

Contents

Acknowledgments

I want to thank the people who guided me through the research for this project. Karen O'Connor, the founder of the Women & Politics Institute at American University, handed me a jumbo storage container filled with books about the suffrage movement, a fraction of the library she has accumulated since being told as a grade schooler that there were no great women leaders. Ann Lewis, a longtime political activist who helped elect Hillary Clinton to the U.S. Senate and who works with the Democratic National Committee to develop women leaders, shared her extensive collection of suffrage writings and memorabilia, along with her wisdom and homemade bread. Brian McLaughlin, reference librarian for the U.S. Senate, unearthed "The Olivia Letters," a collection of writings by journalist Emily Briggs that describe in witty and colorful language the encounters between suffrage leaders and official Washington in the post-Civil War period. Visiting the Sewall-Belmont House on Capitol Hill, where Alice Paul once lived, allowed me to summon up the ghosts of the suffragists as I pored through the yellowed newspaper clippings documenting their struggle. Executive Director Angela Gilchrist and Woman's Party head Marty Langlen welcomed this project, and librarian Jennifer Spencer put just the right books and articles into my hands. Allida Black and Marjorie Lightman, who serve on the Sewall-Belmont Scholars Committee, were generous with their time and advice, as was Jean Baker, a professor of history at Goucher College.

I consulted many books. Two stand out because they provided the road map for the seventy-two-year suffrage struggle. They are *Not for Ourselves Alone: The Story of Elizabeth Cady Stanton and Susan B. Anthony,* which accompanied the Ken Burns documentary on these two women, and *A History of the American Suffragist,* by Doris Weatherford, published on the 150th anniversary of the convention at Seneca Falls. The books I relied on to enrich the detail around pivotal events and people are: *The Story of Alice Paul and the National Woman's Party,* by Inez Haynes Irwin; *Jailed for Freedom,* by Doris Stevens; and *The Perfect 36: Tennessee Delivers Woman Suffrage* by Carol Lynn Yellin and Janann Sherman. John Roberts's seminal new work on the political influence of first ladies arrived while I was writing and proved a valuable resource for historical context and sweep. His *Rating the First Ladies: The Women Who Influence the Presidency* is a serious treatment of a role traditionally undervalued. My goal was to construct a narrative that has the immediacy of contemporary events. If I succeeded, it is because I was able to build on the foundation laid by these and other authors.

Finally, I want to thank my editor, Stephen S. Power, who invited me to undertake this project, and my husband, Tom Brazaitis, who is my first and most faithful reader.

Introduction

Helen Thomas encouraged me to write this book. A media icon whose long career spans nine presidents, Thomas started in journalism writing radio copy during World War II. When the war was over and the men returned home, women were expected to give up their jobs and go back to tending house. Thomas loved the workplace and eventually became the equal of any man as one of the longest-serving and best-known White House correspondents. We were on a panel not long ago speaking to high school students, and Thomas urged the girls never to take their rights for granted. She told them the suffragists marched for thirty years before women got the vote, and that Susan B. Anthony and others were jailed for daring to demand access to the ballot box. "And these are rights we should have been born with," she concluded with gusto. The girls listened wide-eyed as though happening upon this piece of history for the first time. They couldn't imagine a time when women weren't allowed to vote. "Young women today think this all just dropped from the sky," Thomas said with a sigh. "They have no idea how long women struggled."

The Founding Sisters must have been smiling when ten-year-old Mindy Tucker announced with great conviction to her classmates that a woman could be president. Her fifth-grade teacher in Texas, Mr. Clodfelter, a fearsome presence in the classroom, found the assertion so preposterous that at the next parent-teacher conference, he asked the girl's mother where she might have gotten such an outlandish notion. It was 1980, and girls were not encouraged to think of themselves as future presidents. Tucker's mother told him it was her idea. Divorced and with a career of her own, she set the example for her daughter. The next decades brought visible progress for women in all the professions, including politics. By the dawn of the twenty-first century, the prospect of a woman president no longer seemed radical or ridiculous, and girls were increasingly brought up to think of themselves as leaders in the society in addition to homemakers. Tucker became the first female spokesperson at the Justice Department, a job she landed after working in George W. Bush's presidential campaign. She laughs when she recounts her grade-school experience. It seems so remote and unconnected to American life today, when women take their place along with men as senators, Supreme Court justices, presidential advisers, and presidential candidates.

First lady Edith Wilson was among those who found the suffragists "disgusting creatures." She did not hide her disdain for the societal disruption they represented. Yet her reverence for tradition did not stop her from taking over her husband's duties after he suffered a disabling stroke, making her the most powerful woman ever to live in the

White House, while at the same time concealing the true nature of her husband's impairment. She probably saw it less as seizing power than protecting her husband's image, which would fall within the wifely sphere. Women were fearful that suffrage would topple them from their pedestal and thrust them into competition with men for which they were not suited. They worried that by claiming equality they would lose the special protections they enjoyed as the weaker sex. This argument was revisited in more recent times when writer Nora Ephron quipped that the most enduring legacy of the feminist movement was the Dutch treat.

Women are not equal in every respect to men; there are still battles to be fought. But a girl born today begins her journey with an equal sense of possibility for the future. Women are the crown jewel of the electorate. Politicians court their votes; the fabled soccer moms decide elections; and women, if they ever decided to vote as a bloc, could run the country. It was not always this way. When Woodrow Wilson was inaugurated president in March 1913, a married woman was considered the property of her husband. Women couldn't serve on juries or in the event of divorce gain custody of their children. Women couldn't travel alone comfortably. A lone woman staying in a hotel was considered "loose." It was radical thinking to propose that women participate in society directly as individuals rather than as an extension of their husbands or fathers. Opponents of suffrage predicted family life would collapse if women were allowed out of their preordained "sphere" of house and home. Suffrage comes from the

Latin *suffragiem,* or vote, and it was at the heart of the
reform movements that began to take root in America
beginning in the 1890s, during what was known as the
Progressive Era.

Cultural change of this magnitude doesn't occur unless
millions of people come to a consensus that it is needed.
How public opinion was molded and then mobilized to
pass the Nineteenth Amendment to ensure women the
right to vote is the model for the other major social movements of the twentieth century. The future passage of civil
rights legislation in the 1960s, the antiwar protests during
the Vietnam era, and the modern women's movement of
the 1970s all have their roots in the seventy-two-year
battle to win "woman suffrage," as it was called at the
time. What makes the suffrage movement most unlike the
others is that most of its intended beneficiaries for most of
those seven-plus decades did not share its goals. The
majority of women did not particularly care about getting
the vote, or were openly hostile toward suffrage. Women
who wanted the vote were for the longest time in the
minority among women.

My own career parallels the women's movement. I
started at *Newsweek* as a secretary in 1963, with no expec-
tation of becoming a reporter or a writer. With rare exceptions, women at the newsmagazines were confined to
clerical and research positions. I was grateful to work in a
place where what I typed was interesting. When feminist
Gloria Steinem appeared on the cover of *Newsweek* in
March 1970, there was no woman on staff whom the edi-
tors would entrust to write about her. An outsider was

brought in, journalist Helen Dudar, who did a first-rate job interpreting the new feminism sweeping the country as a long-lasting movement with consequences for women and men alike. But the fuse was lit. The women at *Newsweek* brought a class-action suit against the magazine for discrimination. Nora Ephron, a *Newsweek* researcher, was among the plaintiffs. The *Washington Post* owns *Newsweek,* and when publisher Katharine Graham learned of the lawsuit, she asked, "Which side am I supposed to be on?" She was management, but she also was a woman.

The case was settled out of court, and *Newsweek* agreed to a system of goals and timetables to advance women at the magazine. I applied for an internship, and the biggest hurdle I had to get over was convincing the chief of correspondents that I could handle out-of-town assignments because I had young children. Soon after my internship, I was assigned to cover Jimmy Carter's first presidential campaign. When he won, I was named White House correspondent for *Newsweek*. I call it my Cinderella story.

This is the story of the Founding Sisters. They engineered the greatest expansion of democracy on a single day that the world had ever seen, and yet suffrage faded from public memory almost as soon as it happened. The leaders built no monuments to themselves, and they didn't form an organization to give out medals every year. Those who lived to see their vision become a reality returned to their lives much as the women of World War II went back home. Twenty-six million women voted in the presidential election of 1920, most of them echoing the views of the men in their lives. It wasn't until 1980 and the election of

Ronald Reagan that the political parties recognized the potential of women as an independent voting force. Wary of Reagan's cowboy image, women did not embrace the former actor with the same exuberance as men, giving rise to the gender gap that has been a feature of American politics ever since.

1

Stirrings of Discontent

Early grumblings among women over their second-class status surfaced during colonial times when Abigail Adams implored her husband and future president John Adams to "remember the ladies and be more favorable to them than your ancestors." Adams was meeting with the Continental Congress in Philadelphia when Abigail wrote him in March 1776 from their farm near Boston to urge that any new code of laws drafted along with the Declaration of Independence put women on a more equal footing. "Do not put such unlimited power into the hands of husbands," she pleaded. "Remember all men would be tyrants if they could. If particular care and attention are not paid to the ladies, we are determined to foment a rebellion and will not hold ourselves bound to obey any laws in which we have no voice or representation. That your sex are naturally tyrannical is a truth so thoroughly established as to admit of no dispute, but such of you as wish to be happy willingly give up the harsh title of master for the more tender and endearing one of friend."

Though Adams recognized that his wife's superior business sense allowed him the luxury of a life in politics, he didn't take seriously the yearnings she expressed. He was bemused by her letter, and presumed that somebody must have planted these strange thoughts in her head. He didn't even try to humor her. "Depend on it," he wrote back. "We know better than to repeal our masculine systems." There was no women's movement during the Revolutionary period to apply pressure on the Founding Fathers. Maybe we can credit pillow talk for the gender-neutral language in the Declaration of Independence. The promise of "life, liberty, and the pursuit of happiness" and a government that derives power from "the consent of the governed" did not exclude women. To the contrary, it established democratic principles upon which the suffrage movement was based.

The early suffragists were abolitionists, and the drive to end slavery became linked in the public mind with agitation for women's civil rights. Women abolitionists crossed the ocean to attend the World Anti-Slavery Convention in June 1840. Among the delegates was twenty-five-year-old Elizabeth Cady Stanton, who was attending with her journalist husband, Henry. They had just gotten married the previous month and were on their honeymoon. Filled with the idealism of youth and brimming with ideas, Elizabeth Stanton expected to fully participate in this intellectual assemblage of world leaders. She wrote later how chagrined she was to discover that American clergymen, who had landed a few days earlier, had been "busily engaged in fanning the English prejudice into active hostility against the admission of these women into the Convention." The women argued that a country governed by Queen Victoria surely wouldn't exclude them; their opponents pointed out with equal certitude that the queen had sent a man, Prince Albert, to convey her antislavery views instead of appearing herself. A vote on whether to seat the female delegates lost by a decisive margin, and the women were relegated to an area behind a curtain, where they could hear what was going on but would not be visible.

Stanton was outraged by the treatment. She had been rebelling against the boundaries imposed on her gender since she was a child. One of eleven children, she had seen several of her siblings die before reaching adulthood, not an uncommon experience in the days before vaccines and antibiotics. Four of her five brothers died when they were children, and the fifth passed away when he was twenty years old. Her father was overcome with grief, and the young Elizabeth would climb into his lap in an effort to comfort him. What he said would shape her life, and her life's work. "Oh my darling, I wish you were a boy." She tried hard to fill the void in his life, promising, "I will try to be all the boy my brother was." There was no endeavor that was off-limits in her mind because of her gender. She learned to ride a horse and jump high fences as adeptly as any boy. She won a Latin competition and became so skilled at oratory that her father worried she was getting too good at tasks meant for men, a stigma that could make her less appealing as a wife.

Stanton worked for fifty years to see that women could vote, and she died before it happened. What sustained her that day in 1840 as she sat behind the curtain was a vision of what was possible, if women would only demand their fair share. Stanton didn't worry about social conventions. She had persuaded her husband to omit the traditional bride's vow of obedience from their wedding ceremony. Sitting cordoned off like some alien species made her angry, and as women tend to do, Stanton found a soulmate. Before long, she and Lucretia Mott of Philadelphia, who was a generation older and a battle-hardened veteran of the abolitionist wars, abandoned the convention and spent much of their time haranguing the male delegates staying at their hotel for their undemocratic behavior. The two women vowed to convene a woman's rights convention once they returned home to America.

Eight years passed before the promise they made to each other on a long walk in one of London's parks would become a reality. Life got in the way. Stanton had given birth to the first three of her seven children, while her husband studied law with her father, who was a judge in Johnstown, New York. After Henry Stanton passed the bar, the family moved to Boston, where Elizabeth thrived in the cosmopolitan atmosphere. Henry longed for a less competitive environment, and in 1847 the couple moved to Seneca Falls, New York, a sleepy upstate community where he could establish a law practice of his own without fear of competition. Elizabeth missed her activist Boston friends, and was miserable in Seneca Falls.

In one of those fateful moments of history, who should materialize at the same time in this out-of-the-way western New York town than Lucretia Mott. Her youngest sister lived in the area and was pregnant with her seventh child. Mott had come to visit, pleased that despite the numerous pregnancies, her sister clung to unconventional ideas, teaching her sons needlework, and bragging that one had knit a bag for his marbles. At an afternoon tea at the home of a mutual acquaintance, Stanton and Mott renewed their friendship and revived their call for a woman's convention. Egged on by the other women there, all Quaker activists like Mott, they took action that very afternoon in 1848, composing the notice that would appear a few days later in the *Seneca County Courier* and launch the long campaign to win woman suffrage:

WOMAN'S RIGHTS CONVENTION—A Convention to discuss the social, civil, and religious condition and rights of women, will be held in the Wesleyan Chapel, at Seneca Falls, New York, on Wednesday and Thursday, the nineteenth and 20th of July, current; commencing at 10 o'clock A.M. During the first day the meeting will be exclusively for women, who are earnestly invited to attend. The public generally are invited to be present on the second day, when Lucretia Mott, of Philadelphia, and other ladies and gentlemen, will address the convention.

The Sunday morning before the convention, the women gathered in the parlor of one of the local Quaker women activists to draft the program. First they pored over papers from the numerous meetings they had attended having to do with ending slavery, banning alcohol, and promoting peace. None seemed right for the far-reaching changes they sought in the status of women. They decided to think really big, so they took as their model the Declaration of Independence, which had been written seventy-two years earlier, in 1776. Little did they know it would be another seventy-two years before their Declaration of Sentiments would be fulfilled, or they might not have been so giddy with enthusiasm as they struck the words "the present King of Great Britain" as the purveyor of tyranny and substituted "all men."

Some three hundred people showed up at the Wesleyan Chapel on the morning of July 19, quite a large number considering it was a weekday, when people had chores to tend to, and Seneca Falls's population was only eight thousand. The organizers had a last-minute moment of panic when they discovered the doors were locked and they were without a key. One of Stanton's nephews had to be boosted through a window to unlock the chapel. So many women had gotten their husbands to hitch up the horses to bring them to town that an unexpectedly large number of men were present. The leaders decided on the spot to let the men attend the first day's proceedings, overruling their own newspaper ad and establishing the important precedent that attitude and outlook, not gender, determine who is a feminist.

Women were unaccustomed in 1848 to any kind of public role. There was a taboo against public speaking by women, and there were no women's organizations of any consequence yet where women could learn the skills of running a meeting according to parliamentary rules.

Overwhelmed by the large crowd they had attracted, Stanton and the others hastily retreated to the altar in the church, where they held a quick meeting and decided that they would let the experienced men who were there take the lead role. Lucretia Mott's husband, James, presided, dressed in Quaker costume and looking quite dignified. Various women leaders read speeches, but the star of the convention was Frederick Douglass, ten years out of slavery and an imposing figure both physically and intellectually. Douglass stood well over six feet tall at a time when the average man was considerably shorter. He was a formidable lecturer, capable of holding the attention of thousands of people for up to two hours at a time, a far more taxing task on the vocal cords in the days before microphones. He could command $100 for a lecture, a huge sum at the time. The speaking fees he earned eventually made him a rich man, and he delighted in displaying crystal and fine china in his home.

Douglass provided a charismatic presence at Seneca Falls that helped offset the ridicule aimed at the women who attended "The Hen Convention," as it was popularly dubbed. One newspaper writer described the women as "divorced wives, childless women, and some old maids." The widely held view that women agitating for rights were life's losers served as a powerful deterrent against women openly declaring themselves in favor of women's rights. If a woman's role was solely to bear and nurture children, then these women were society's misfits. The women themselves were divided over how far they legitimately could go without being totally dismissed as wackos, and couldn't agree on whether to include a demand for the ballot on their list of grievances. Stanton favored it; Mott opposed, fearing that suffrage was so wild an idea that it would undermine any credibility the fledgling women's movement had. Stanton's husband, a radical reformer in his own right, told her that if she supported a woman's right to vote, he would be so embarrassed that he would have to leave town. She did, and he did, but only for the duration of the convention.

Douglass sided with Stanton, making the case that the right to participate in government is a fundamental principle of equality, from which all other rights would flow. The Stanton-Douglass position carried by a small majority. But when the final document was voted on after two days of debate, the resolution calling for the right to vote was the only one of a dozen resolutions that did not pass unanimously. For those with a looking glass into the future, that signaled the difficulty ahead when women activists and their male sympathizers could not fully agree that the ballot was necessary. For the ordinary rank and file of women, it would be decades before even a majority of them would favor suffrage.

With much work left undone and their enthusiasms unleashed, Stanton and the others arranged for a follow-up meeting in two weeks in Rochester, New York. They placed a notice in the daily newspapers, and once again so many women showed up that the Unitarian church where the meeting was held was filled to overflowing. This time the women did not shrink from their role as leaders. Though James Mott was there and volunteered to preside, the women ran the meeting. Some had never spoken in public before and had difficulty summoning the vocal power needed to be heard by everyone in the church. There were repeated cries of "Louder! Louder!" but the women didn't back down. It was an exercise in survival of the fittest until a handful of women emerged with the ability to project themselves well enough to be heard. Perhaps because the setting was a church, much of the discussion centered on the biblical interpretation of a woman's place. Stanton pointed out that nowhere in the Bible does it dictate a woman should take her husband's name.

Spurred on by the large turnout, the women grew bolder and more concrete in their actions. The first resolution they adopted called for the vote; another commended Elizabeth Blackwell, the first woman admitted to a traditional medical school. In contrast to the lofty calls for equality issued at Seneca Falls, the Rochester convention focused on bread-and-butter issues: the inheritance rights of widows, property ownership, and the right of women to keep the money they earned. Women had almost no status in the eyes of the law. Granting a husband the legal right to his wife's earnings reduces her "almost to the condition of a slave," the conventioneers declared, a statement meant to solidify the bonds between women's aspirations and the growing abolitionist movement in America. Douglass was there to lend his considerable moral stature to the fight.

Susan B. Anthony, a stern and stubborn schoolteacher, read news reports about the conventions. She did not attend either of them, and had no intention of becoming an activist. She backed the call for better education and more equal economic opportunity, but she balked at the demand for the ballot. She was a Quaker and a pacifist and believed it was wrong to cast a vote for any government that would go to war. Her father did not vote until 1860, when he was confronted with conflicting moral priorities. Because he was convinced that war was the only way to rid the country of slavery, he voted for Abraham Lincoln. Born on February 15, 1820, Susan B. Anthony displayed an independent streak from an early age. When a teacher in elementary school told her long division was only for boys ("A girl needs to know how to read her Bible and count her egg money, nothing more"), Anthony worked out a compromise that allowed her to sit behind the teacher and take notes. In an era when few women worked outside the home, Anthony had taken a teaching job to help support her family. Her father had gone bankrupt in 1837, the result of a collapse in land speculation.

This first national depression provided opportunities for women like Anthony who might otherwise never have created a household separate from their father's. Anthony spent more than a decade as a teacher, and there were few hints that she would go on to become the woman most identified with the drive to gain women the vote. At the time of the Seneca Falls and Rochester conventions, she was twenty-eight, unmarried, and extremely skeptical about suffrage. On a visit home to Rochester, she was surprised to learn that her father, mother, and younger sister, Mary—shy and unassertive and hardly typical of the stereotypical suffragist—all had attended the Rochester meeting and signed the resolutions, including the demand for equal suffrage. They were enthused by the experience and eager to share the inside gossip about how Stanton and Mott lobbied to have Douglass chair the convention because they were worried the women weren't up to the task and would cause embarrassment that could derail the fledgling movement. When several women threatened to go home if they didn't get leadership roles, Stanton and Mott relented.

Anthony found the tales of the suffrage sisters amusing, but she was drawn more to the growing temperance movement. Liquor was making women's lives hell. The degree of alcoholism in the country was extraordinarily high, and with it came violence, much of it expressed against women in domestic situations in their own homes. It seemed that almost all men drank immoderately, which some social historians speculate was the result of some 228 years of Puritanism, since the founding of the colonies, where anything joyful was associated with sin. Singing, dancing, card-playing, outdoor sports, even the boisterous play of children were frowned on. Many working men found escape in alcohol; for whatever reason, women typically did not seek the same relief, and instead bore the brunt of their husbands' inability to control either their drinking or their temper. Anthony was active in the local chapter of the Daughters of Temperance in the small town of Canajoharie in central New York State, where she was teaching, and began to devote much of her time to the cause. She organized supper events to raise money ("One dollar will admit a gentleman and a lady."), and on weekends traveled to nearby towns and villages to help found additional women's chapters. She tried to persuade the Sons of Temperance, mostly reformed "old soaks" and pious clergymen, that women could play a key role in the movement.

Women brought far more energy and commitment to the cause, and when the New York Sons of Temperance held a convention of all the state chapters in January 1852 in Albany, they invited the women's branches to send delegates. Anthony attended as a representative of the Rochester Daughters of Temperance. She and the other women delegates were seated along with the men in the convention hall, which presented a visual image of equality. But when Anthony rose to speak, the chairman cut her off, telling her the women were there to listen and to learn but not to speak. No one had worked harder than she gathering the petitions calling on the state legislature to pass a law that would ban the sale and production of liquor. Indignant at being ignored, Anthony walked out, trailed by several equally irate women.

Anthony was an imposing woman whose physical presence could be intimidating. At five feet, six inches, she was tall for her day, but it was her leanness and sharp features that made her appear all angles, especially when contrasted with the woman who would become her best friend and soulmate. Elizabeth Cady Stanton was as round and cheery as Anthony was trim and serious. Though Anthony would become "Aunt Susan" to generations of suffragists, her plain looks and dark hair pulled back tightly over her ears into a bun gave no hint then of her charisma as a leader and the pivotal role she would play in history. Inflamed by the men who had spurned her talents, men she called "white orthodox male saints," Anthony went directly from the Sons of Temperance convention to the *Albany Evening Journal*. She persuaded a sympathetic editor to do a story on how the women had been shut out, and to urge interested citizens to come hear her and the other women delegates the next day at the local Presbyterian church.

The circumstances were less than ideal. Outside, a wicked snowstorm blanketed the area; inside, a balky chimney filled the meeting room with smoke, and a stovepipe crashed to the floor in the midst of the program. But the women forged ahead, resolving to convene their own Women's State Temperance Convention, and to hell with the men. Anthony almost single-handedly raised the money, hired the hall, arranged for speakers, and wrote the hundreds of letters of invitation such an undertaking required in the days before e-mail and faxes. She asked her new friend Stanton, whose lively intelligence she admired, to be a featured speaker. The two women had met the previous spring when a mutual friend, Amelia Bloomer, editor of a temperance monthly, *The Lily,* introduced them in Seneca Falls, where they had both attended a lecture by William Lloyd Garrison, a prominent abolitionist and staunch ally of women's suffrage. Bloomer's name (or rather her husband's name) became synonymous with the trousers that suffragists had begun wearing, which Bloomer had publicized in her journal. A cousin of Stanton's had developed the simpler way to dress in order to be comfortable while she gardened and tended her young children. An envious Stanton watched her cousin maneuver effortlessly while she struggled with the required corset, layers of petticoats, and floor-length dress that women of her station were expected to wear. Stanton was sold on the freedom the simplified garb offered, and wore the new look to the 1852 and 1853 meetings of the Women's State Temperance Society. Her husband was horrified when he saw his wife wearing baggy pants under a loose-fitting short dress that ended four inches below the knee. He worried that when the women sat onstage their legs would be exposed above the knees (albeit covered by fabric), and men in the audience could tell "whether their lady friends have round and plump legs, or lean and scrawny ones." But Stanton loved the ease of movement, and adopted dress reform as a symbol of women's independence. "Depend on it," she told her friend Lucretia Mott. "Woman can never develop in her present drapery. She is a slave to her rags."

Women wearing pants took on enormous significance, threatening the entire social order and inviting ridicule in much the same way that feminists more than a century later became the objects of scorn for burning their bras and refusing to shave their legs. Stanton's father told her she was not welcome in his house wearing such an outfit, and her sons, who were away at boarding school, pleaded with her to wear something else when she visited. Anthony had reluctantly adopted the new look. She cared nothing for fashion, and agreed at first only to placate Stanton. Lucy Stone, a teacher and early ally of Anthony and Stanton, described being surrounded on a New York street and jeered by "a wall of men and boys" because the women were wearing the short dress that identified them as "ultras," the most radical wing of the suffrage movement. By early 1854, after they had made their point, most women quietly returned to conventional dress rather than put up with the constant harassment. Anthony was one of the last holdouts. Having committed herself to the cause of dress reform, she hated surrendering the principle even though she realized how divisive and diversionary the short dress had become. Stanton kept after the hardheaded Anthony. "Let the hem of your dress out today," Stanton urged. "The cup of ridicule is greater than you can bear. It is not wise, Susan, to use up so much energy in that way."

Anthony finally relented, explaining that the short dress had become "an intellectual slavery." For somebody like her, who despised the frivolous focus on self, she couldn't bear the knowledge that audiences were more interested in her clothes than her words.

The five hundred women who gathered for the Women's State Temperance Convention in Rochester, New York, on April 20, 1852, chose Anthony as their secretary and Stanton as their president, a division of labor that represented the complementary talents of these two women, who would remain lifelong friends until Stanton's death in 1902. Stanton's inaugural speech was a blockbuster. She advocated divorce to end marriages plagued by drunkenness, with custody of any children to the mother, and said women should refuse to bear the children of a drunkard. Divorce was a taboo subject at the time, and nobody in polite society talked about birth control, though there were quack remedies available, and thinly veiled newspaper advertisements for abortionists. Anthony was enthralled by Stanton's ability to convey her convictions with such clarity and eloquence, and began spending a great deal of time at Stanton's home in Seneca Falls.

Anthony was thirty-three and Stanton was thirty-eight when they began their collaboration. They came from different backgrounds and had radically opposite dispositions, but they were fearless about where they were going and what they wanted. Their shared goal bonded them for half a century. Stanton was already drifting into matronhood and had begun wearing a cap, as though to conceal the thinning hair of old age. Anthony was seen as an "old maid," the moniker given any unmarried woman over age thirty. Stanton had been born an aristocrat. Her father, a noted judge who also had served in Congress, had grudging admiration for her "masculine mind," which showed in her confident manner and facility at quick repartee. But he did not believe in women participating in public life and opposed her at every turn, even threatening to disinherit her when she got out of hand. Anthony's father, Daniel, a devout Quaker, encouraged his daughter and even offered to bankroll her activities once he recovered financially from the economic depression of 1837. Teachers then "boarded round," which meant staying in a series of cramped rooms with various farm families and having no private life. Anthony understood what it was like to work for a living, which Stanton, coming from a more privileged family, knew only in theory. "In thought and sympathy we were

one, and in the division of labor we exactly comple-
mented each other," Stanton said of their collaboration.
"In writing we did better work than either could do alone.
While she is slow and analytic in composition I am rapid
and synthetic. I am the better writer, the better critic. She
supplied the facts and statistics, I the philosophy and rhetoric. . . . Our speeches may be considered the joint products of our two brains."

When the Men's State Temperance Society held their next
convention, in Syracuse, Anthony's organization was once
again invited to send delegates. Anthony was ecstatic, certain that the men had seen the light. But when she and
Mrs. Bloomer arrived in Syracuse, they were told that the
other delegates, most of them ministers and members of
the clergy, objected to having them there, and they would
have to leave. The women refused. So the clergymen railed
on about the nerve of these women to crash men's meetings, and to confuse the high moral calling of temperance
with crass appeals for women's rights such as divorce and
"free love," and who knows what else. Angry clergy
denounced the women as "a hybrid species, half man and
half woman, belonging to neither sex." Anthony stood her
ground, pointing out over howls of protest that more than
a hundred thousand women had signed petitions for a
prohibition law in Maine the previous winter. Still, the
experience shook her to the core and made her question
whether more radical steps were needed.

Maybe Anthony's temperance crusade didn't address the

basic ills of society. More and more, she used her speeches to argue for women's rights. Her father's farm on the out-skirts of Rochester had become a center of progressive activity. Among the regular visitors was Frederick Douglass, whose newspaper the *North Star* was edited in Rochester. Douglass was an outspoken defender of women's rights in addition to being a leading abolitionist, and on visits home, Anthony came to realize that the causes of fighting slavery and supporting suffrage were one. At about the same time, her temperance activities began to falter. A little-noticed clause in the constitution for the Women's State Temperance Society that she and Stanton had founded the previous year, in 1852, allowed men as members but lim-ited officeholders to women. Many of the traditional women members and, of course, most of the men thought this was an unconscionable abridgment of men's liberties, and Stanton, as president, yielded to their way of thinking even as she feared the consequences. The result was pre-dictable: the men quickly dominated all the proceedings, struck gender from the society's name, calling it The Peo-ple's League, and booted Stanton from the presidency. They reelected Anthony as secretary, but she declined the honor, preferring instead to resign, in solidarity with Stan-ton. Within two years, the society disbanded. But the expe-rience was a revelation for Anthony.

"Do you see, at last?" Stanton said to her. Stanton believed all along that women must first gain their rights, and had joined the temperance crusade more out of loyalty to Anthony than conviction.

"At last, I see," Anthony replied.

2

"Ain't I a Woman?"

A former slave named Sojourner Truth electrified a woman's rights convention in Akron, Ohio, in 1851, striding to the front of the crowd through a raucous band of clergymen who were determined to disrupt the meeting. More than six feet tall and built like a halfback with huge muscles from working in the fields, Truth ridiculed the argument that women were too delicate to survive outside the protection of the home and should be shielded from public life. "The man over there says women need to be helped into carriages and lifted over ditches, and to have the best place everywhere. Nobody ever helps me into carriages or over puddles, or gives me the best place— and ain't I a woman?" She flexed her arm to show her strength and said, "I could work as much and eat as much as a man—when I could get it—and bear the lash as well! And ain't I a woman? I have borne thirteen children, and seen most of 'em sold into slavery, and when I cried out with my mother's grief, none but Jesus heard me—and ain't I a woman?"

"And this thing in the head—what do they call it?" Somebody cried out "Intellect!" as Truth reminded the clergymen that Jesus was the product of God and a woman; man had nothing to do with it. By the time she finished, even some of the clergymen were applauding. Her speech was never written down at the time, but it survived because it was so memorable. Supporters of slavery and antisuffrage sympathizers tried to undermine her credibility by claiming that she was really a man. What else could explain her deep, resonant voice? To disabuse these critics, Truth announced that as a slave she had suckled many white babies, sometimes to the exclusion of her own children. According to a report published in the *Liberator,* William Lloyd Garrison's abolitionist newspaper, before one particularly hostile audience in Indiana, she disrobed, flaunted her breasts, and asked if anybody present wished to partake. "It was not to her shame that she uncovered her breast before them, but to their shame," the paper noted.

Truth was born a slave named Isabella in the 1790s in New York and escaped in the 1820s to find refuge first in New York City, and then in a utopian commune in western Massachusetts, where she became part of a network of reformers. She gained legal freedom under an 1817 New York statute that freed slaves under forty in the year 1827. Though she could neither read nor write, she was unmatched as a storyteller. Her autobiography, *Narrative of Sojourner Truth: A Northern Slave,* which she dictated, details the physical deprivation and the emotional abuse she endured as the property of slaveowners. "She's the Oprah of her day," says historian Allida Black. Truth had no permanent address and supported herself as a live-in domestic. When she traveled, she stayed with leaders of the woman's movement, including Anthony and Stanton. When the Civil War broke out, Truth became a fixture at prounion rallies in the North. She had a great sense of theatricality. Dressed in red, white, and blue, she transfixed audiences with her physical presence and her spellbinding oratory.

The moral responsibility to speak out against the evils of slavery prompted more women, white and black, to enter public life. Together they drove the reform movement. Harriet Tubman, another escaped slave, put together a network of like-minded individuals to help runaway slaves gain freedom that became known as the Underground Railroad. Her contacts in the southern states were so extensive that when the Civil War broke out, the Union Army used her as a scout and unofficial spy. In June 1863, Tubman escorted a band of black soldiers up the Combahee River in South Carolina and watched with satisfaction as they burned plantations and freed more than eight hundred slaves. As a "conductor" on the Underground Railroad, Tubman made nineteen round trips in ten years, secreting herself and her human cargo in the homes of sympathetic Quakers, and personally escorting three hundred slaves to freedom. The white South put a bounty of $40,000 on her head, which went uncollected. After the war, Tubman appealed to the U.S. Congress to cover the expenses for a trip she had taken to Hilton Head, South Carolina, to gather military intelligence. Congress granted her $20 a month as a pension, but she was already eighty years old at the time.

Skin color didn't matter in the context of fighting slavery. A February 1844 antislavery fair organized by women to raise money for the cause attracted women with bedrock New England names, whose parents fought in the American Revolution. As they sold their homemade jams and jellies, the women shared their discontent at being relegated to the sidelines of society. They came from revolutionary stock. Yet they were denied the right to vote, while all sorts of riffraff, from drunken laborers to untutored immigrants, were welcomed at voting places. Where was the morality in that? Many had come to the unhappy realization that the conditions that limited them as women weren't that different from what slaves experienced. Mary Chesnut, the wife of a slaveowner, wrote in her diary: "[T]here is no slave, after all, like a wife. You know how women sell themselves and are sold in marriage, from queens downward. Poor women, poor slaves."

The fight for suffrage had all the twists and turns of a modern thriller. There was racial conflict as the movement divided over whether to support the extension of the vote to Negroes after slavery was ended. A deal made with President Lincoln to push for woman suffrage at the conclusion of the Civil War collapsed when Lincoln was assassinated. The early suffragists were abolitionists, but their frustration at being excluded from the vote while uneducated blacks were granted suffrage led them to accommodate racist views in an effort to win southern political support. The waves of new immigrants coming into the country were equally problematical for the suffragists. Anti-Irish, anti-Catholic, and antiforeign attitudes took hold as the country industrialized and millions of people arrived each year from cultures considered alien. Most of the men arriving by the boatload were never going to be allies; they held conservative views of women and were deeply distrustful of the suffragists.

An 1853 convention on women's rights in New York attracted women from eleven states and as far away as England and Germany. Admission to the Broadway Tabernacle was twenty-five cents, and every one of the three thousand seats was filled. But not everybody supported women's rights. A number of men had infiltrated the proceedings and did their best to disrupt the speakers, shouting insults and making loud hissing noises. Male speakers, including the noted abolitionist William Lloyd Garrison, were treated with the same disrespect as the women orators. It took Sojourner Truth to put the protestors in their place. "Some of you have got the spirit of a goose, and some have got the spirit of a snake." She spat out the sibilant words, commiserating with her tormentors that they had to endure seeing a colored woman get up and tell them about women's rights. "We'll have our rights," she declared. "You may hiss as much as you like, but it is coming."

Anthony watched in awe as Truth rose above the commonality of the moment. She "combined in herself as an individual the two most hated elements of humanity. She was black, and she was a woman, and all the insults that could be cast upon color and sex were together hurled at her," Anthony wrote. "But there she stood, calm and dignified, a grand wise woman who could neither read nor write, and yet with deep insight could penetrate the very soul of the universe about her."

The event was recorded in feminist history as "the Mob Convention." *New York Tribune* editor Horace Greeley, who welcomed news about women's rights and took the issue seriously, observed in an editorial, "[I]t was evident that if any rowdies had an ant-hole in the bottom of his boot, he would inevitably have sunk through it and disappeared forever." Greeley proved himself a friend of the suffrage movement in its early days, but even he began to have qualms. Where he had once opened the pages of his newspaper to opinion pieces by Stanton, he now couldn't abide her radicalism. The break came over divorce reform. Stanton argued that since marriage was a civil contract, divorce should be a civil right. Even Anthony, Stanton's most loyal friend, didn't want to get sidetracked into a battle over divorce.

At the same time, the abolitionist movement was gaining momentum. Compared to fighting slavery, agitating for women's rights seemed petty and self-involved. Harriet Beecher Stowe's book *Uncle Tom's Cabin,* published in 1852, became an instant best-seller and generated widespread outrage over the institution of slavery. Originally written in serial episodes for a magazine, Stowe's vivid depiction of the long-suffering slave Uncle Tom and the villainous Simon Legree rallied the North to the antislavery movement and gained Stowe an audience with President Lincoln in 1861, soon after he took office. The book personalized the plight of human beings subjected to subhuman conditions, and more than any single event transformed the mounting tension between the North and the South into a moral conflict over slavery. The book was the match that ignited smoldering resentments into a bonfire. Stowe's work documenting the dreary life of frontier women was not nearly so marketable. She wrote this letter to her husband, Calvin, in the late 1830s: "It is a dark, sloppy, muddy, disagreeable day and I have been working hard, washing dishes, looking into closets, and seeing a great deal of the dark side of domestic life. . . . I am sick of the smell of sour milk, and sour meat, and sour everything, and then the clothes will not dry, and no wet thing does, and everything smells moldy; and altogether I feel as if I never wanted to eat again."

In the decade leading up to the Civil War, women struggled against a rising tide of male resistance. The abolitionist debate dominated private and public discussion, obscuring other concerns. There was no audience for women's rights as the nation prepared for war, a reality that Anthony found frustrating at times. She wrote in her journal during this period that she joined a sewing society in an effort to usefully fill her time, but found the company intellectually lacking. She wished that the revolutionary fervor of the abolitionist movement would spread to women, who for the most part remained docile and accepting about their secondary status. The Quaker meetings that once provided her inspiration she now felt offered "too much namby-pambyism." Though her public activism was subdued, she remained involved where she could. Next to an entry in her journal noting that she "washed every window in the house today," Anthony wrote with the same elliptical precision: "Fitted out a fugitive slave for Canada with the help of Harriet Tubman."

Stanton was enmeshed in domesticity, and that created tension with the unmarried Anthony, who was a much freer woman. It irritated Anthony that her friend kept on having children, seven in all, and the children delighted in tormenting this gray ghost of a visitor who would descend on them from time to time. A horrified Anthony would recount stories about schemes perpetrated by the older Stanton boys. She recalled strolling with Stanton only to look up and see the children on the roof debating whether the baby would bounce if dropped.

Stanton held firm to her ideals, often at great emotional cost. Her husband was disturbed by her activism, and blamed her for causing him political embarrassment. Her father, whose encouragement she longed for, threatened to cut her out of his will. "I never felt more keenly the degradation of my sex," she wrote to Anthony. "To think that all in me of which my father would have felt a proper pride had I been a man is deeply mortifying to him because I am a woman." On February 14, 1854, defying both her husband and father, Stanton delivered a stinging speech aimed directly at the men in the New York legislature, which was in session just a few blocks away. She likened the lawmakers to feudal barons in the way they elevated themselves and forced women to "become the ignoble, servile, cringing slave." Anthony had fifty thousand copies of the speech printed to distribute around the state "like flakes of snow," including one on each legislator's desk. But the lawmakers were unmoved. The chairman of the Senate Judiciary Committee announced in a tone heavy with contempt that the men, based on their experience in married life, would take no action. He said "the ladies always have the best place and choicest tid-bit at the table . . . the best seats on the carts, carriage and sleighs . . . their choice on which side of the bed they will lie. . . . If there is any inequality or oppression," he concluded, "the gentlemen are the sufferers."

Anthony had spent five months, much of it in the dead of winter, visiting every one of New York's fifty-four counties, giving speeches and collecting signatures. The Judiciary Committee chairman, noting that some of the petitions bore the names of husband and wife, suggested that these spouses apply for a law to authorize them to change dress, "that the husband may wear petticoats and the wife the breeches." Anthony attracted good-sized crowds wherever she went, in part because a woman speaking publicly was an oddity in 1854, and people were curious. She drove herself to the extent of her physical endurance, insisting that she never missed her morning sponge bath, even when she stayed in unheated country inns and there was nothing but ice water in the pitcher. She arranged to have herself carried in and out of one meeting rather than cancel the event because she had hurt her back.

Perhaps because she was capable of such stoicism and commitment, Anthony had little tolerance for those whose dedication faltered under the weight of love and marriage.

She did not conceal her disappointment when her friend Lucy Stone said she planned to marry. The two were roughly the same age (Anthony was born on February 15, 1820; Stone on August 13, 1818) and shared confidences about their status as single women, pledging to each other that they would forever remain free souls. Stone had graduated from Oberlin College, the country's first college to admit both women and blacks, where she was a star student and was asked to write the commencement speech for her class of 1847. She refused because as a woman, she would not have been permitted to deliver the speech herself. She went on to become a riveting speaker for both abolition and women's rights. Anthony credited a speech she read that Stone had delivered at a woman's convention in 1850 with converting her to the cause of women's rights.

Stone never tiptoed around what she thought. She reveled in controversy. It became customary for male protesters to denounce her by burning pepper in the auditoriums when she spoke, or to hurl prayer books at the stage to express their unhappiness at her unconventional views. But in 1853, in her mid-thirties and an outspoken opponent of marriage, she met Henry Blackwell, and she was smitten. Blackwell was a businessman seven years her junior and an activist in the abolition movement. He courted her for two years, finally winning her over with a demonstration of his moral fiber by rescuing a fugitive slave. The Fugitive Slave Law required residents of nonslaveholding states in the North to return escaped slaves to their owners. The law was widely disregarded, which meant that many law-abiding citizens such as Blackwell routinely risked government penalties to uphold what they believed was the higher principle of opposing slavery. The citizen action during this period provided the moral and intellectual template for the civil disobedience that became a popularly accepted tactic more than a hundred years later, during the civil rights movement.

At their wedding ceremony in 1855, the minister read a statement composed by the couple in which Henry renounced all the privileges of husbandhood that the law conferred upon him, and Lucy announced that she would keep her own name. "A wife should no more take her husband's name than he should hers," said Stone. "My name is my identity and must not be lost." This was a radical step, and Stone would encounter resistance from various authorities for the rest of her life. Some of her furniture was confiscated when she refused to pay taxes on her home, which she argued was taxation without representation, since the property was in her name, and as a woman she could not vote. On legal documents and when she traveled, her signature typically would not be recognized as valid unless she appended it with "married to Harry Blackwell." Though Stone remained just as committed to woman's rights, Anthony felt betrayed, and the tension between them foreshadowed a major break in the suffrage movement.

War was on the horizon, and Anthony didn't think much of the country's new president. Illinois lawyer Abraham Lincoln was elected in November 1860 on a pledge to stop the spread of slavery, but he made no promises about ending the abhorrent practice where it already existed.

Anthony was a Quaker pacifist. She didn't like the war talk; but she didn't like Lincoln's equivocation, either. She thought he was just another dissembling politician who could not be trusted to do the right thing. But to the South, Lincoln's election was the equivalent of an ultimatum to end slavery. South Carolina seceded from the Union before Lincoln was even sworn in, with Georgia, Alabama, and other Dixie states following. On April 12, 1861, only days after Lincoln's inauguration (presidents then were inaugurated in March; a 1933 constitutional amendment moved the date to January), Southerners attacked Fort Sumter, a federal military post off the coast of Charleston, South Carolina. Lincoln had two choices: he could accept the secession of the eleven states that had bound together in the Confederacy; or he could fight to preserve the Union. He wrote in a letter to the journalist Horace Greeley that his goal was to preserve the Union, and if that required the abolition of slavery, so be it. And so began the Civil War, an event of such overwhelming significance to the country that everything else seemed trivial by comparison.

Stanton urged Anthony to cancel the Woman's Rights Convention planned for the following month in New York. Attendance would be down, and to go ahead seemed less than loyal, Stanton said. Anthony feared that the moment women dropped their guard, the powers that be would reverse the modest gains they had made.

She reluctantly agreed to put off the convention. Soon after, with the country plunged into war, the New York legislature repealed one of her most concrete achievements to date, a provision in the Married Woman's Property Act granting mothers equal guardianship of their children. It was futile to press for women's rights in the climate of war, and Anthony threw herself instead into organizing a "no compromise with slavery" tour of upstate New York. It was a total fiasco. In town after town, Anthony and her entourage of well-known abolitionists, including Frederick Douglass, were booed and heckled and pelted with eggs to the point where they couldn't continue. People on both sides of the slavery issue had come to detest the abolitionists, blaming their zealotry for bringing the country to the precipice. A Rome, New York, newspaper called Anthony's road company "pestiferous fanatics." In Utica, the manager of the hall Anthony had rented for $60 barred her from entering. The show went on in Albany, the state capital, thanks to the mayor, who sat on the stage throughout the event, his revolver visible on his lap.

It was a particularly trying time for Stanton. She hadn't traveled much in recent years, and was unaccustomed to being away from her family for such a long period. Her husband pleaded with her to return home. He worried that she and the others were risking their lives. "The mobocrats would as soon kill you as not," he wrote. In addition to his concern about her safety, Henry Stanton had other reasons to want her to cease and desist. He was in Washington trying to ingratiate himself with the new Republican administration, and having a notorious wife on the front lines of the most divisive issue in the country didn't help his résumé. Stanton dismissed her husband's pleadings, but the angry political climate forced an end to their grand antislavery tour. And Henry Stanton managed

to win an appointment as deputy collector at the Customs
House in Manhattan, not a major position but high
enough to keep up his contacts in Washington.

In early 1863 the war was not going well for the
North, and abolitionists were upset that Lincoln had limited his Emancipation Proclamation, issued the previous
September, to freeing slaves in the rebellious Confederacy,
but said nothing about the North. Massachusetts senator
Charles Sumner, a Republican, introduced a constitutional amendment to extend emancipation everywhere. He
needed a two-thirds vote in both houses of Congress
before the amendment could be sent to the states for ratification. Henry Stanton proposed to Anthony and his wife
that they rally women in the North to back the amendment, an offer that both women eagerly accepted.
Together with Lucy Stone, they formed the Women's
National Loyal League, funneling all their activist energy
into an effort that swelled to two thousand volunteers who
ultimately collected four hundred thousand signatures, the
largest campaign of its kind the country had ever seen.
Thanks to their work, Sumner's amendment outlawing
slavery was on its way to become the Thirteenth Amendment to the Constitution.

With Henry Stanton their pipeline to the White House,
Stanton and Anthony extracted a promise from Lincoln that
if they stopped agitating for suffrage during the Civil War,
he would support suffrage after the war was over. But Lincoln was assassinated a few days after the war ended, and his
early plans for the emancipation of slaves did not include
suffrage as part of their newly won freedom. He was very

worried about giving male slaves the right to vote, and had proposed limiting the vote to those who had served in the military and were literate. Andrew Johnson from Tennessee, Lincoln's vice president, was elevated to the presidency. A Democrat and a former slaveholder, Johnson offered little continuity to either the policies or character of the president in whose administration he served. It was not unusual in those days for a president and vice president to come from different parties, but the change infuriated the party of Lincoln. Johnson dragged his feet on Reconstruction, wanting to leave everything in the hands of white Southerners and discrediting Lincoln's legacy in the eyes of Republicans. The result was a seismic shift in the political dynamics of Congress, with radical Republicans taking over. Unlike the modern right-wing activists in the GOP, these radicals were radical to the left, and they moved quickly to impeach Johnson, who had almost no base of support on Capitol Hill. He may have been a slaveholder, but he hated the wealthy planter class, and had little rapport with southern Democrats, the barons of the party.

Johnson survived impeachment by a single vote in the Senate, but he was left powerless. Progressive Republicans were in control in the Senate, and they pushed through the Thirteenth, Fourteenth, and Fifteenth amendments, which consolidated the Union's gains from the Civil War, and taken together represented a huge step forward for democracy. The Thirteenth Amendment ended slavery. The Fourteenth Amendment extended citizenship to slaves and former slaves and created the due process clause, which says nobody can be deprived of life, liberty, or property without due process of law. It was needed at the federal level to override a wave of "Black Codes" being passed in the South that restricted the rights of freed blacks almost to the point of restoring slavery. The Fifteenth Amendment enraged Stanton and Anthony because it gave male former slaves the right to vote, while women were left out. They objected to giving the vote to thousands of uneducated farmhands, black men whom Stanton called "Sambos," while refusing educated white women a voice in the government. Despite their long history as abolitionists, the reaction of Stanton and Anthony to this double standard bore the ugly stain of racism.

At a memorial service for Lincoln, Frederick Douglass shocked the assemblage by describing Lincoln as "preeminently the white man's president, entirely devoted to the welfare of white men." He went on to say that black people, who nonetheless honored Lincoln for what he ultimately did in securing their freedom, showed their gratitude by their willingness to put his failings in perspective.

Lincoln may have fallen short in the eyes of the activists, but the events that he set in motion made him an unqualified hero for future generations of Americans, black and white. Women, however, would have to wait another fifty years before gaining the same voting rights as freed male slaves.

Through the Civil War until the Fourteenth Amendment, the word "male" had never appeared in the U.S. Constitution. Stanton and Anthony waged a valiant campaign to include woman suffrage in the Fourteenth Amendment, which extended citizenship and with it the vote to roughly two million freedmen living in the former Confederacy. They collected 10,000 signatures on petitions, which they brought to Congress and presented to Senator Sumner, who had welcomed their efforts in the past. This time Sumner wanted nothing to do with the women. He pronounced their petition drive "most inopportune," and the Republicans, aligned with the drive to give black men the vote, declined even to put the petitions before Congress.

One of the great moral conflicts of the time—slavery—was about to be resolved, at least on paper, and in the eyes of even the most ardent supporters of woman suffrage, the Negro's claim took priority. Frederick Douglass said there is "no place I can lay this wooly head of mine" except with these women, but he made the case that black Americans need special protection. Rebuffed at every turn and told "This is the Negro's hour," Stanton and Anthony were furious at the way they had been betrayed, and vowed to never again rely on men to advance the cause. But they had few allies, even among women. The result was a bitter split in the movement over race, with Stanton and Anthony forming the National Suffrage Association (NSA) centered in New York and Washington, and Lucy Stone at the head of the more moderate American Woman Suffrage Association (AWSA), which was based in New England. They differed not only over their response to the Fifteenth Amendment, but also in their tactics and approach. The NSA purged all men; even the typesetters who worked on the *Revolution,* a weekly generated by Stanton and Anthony to disseminate their ideas, had to be women. The gentler AWSA had men on its board, and believed suffrage would be better won state-by-state than by appealing to the Congress. Stanton and Anthony didn't have the patience for endless state campaigns; they wanted to keep the heat on Washington.

The rift lasted for twenty years.

3

Testing the Limits

The first convention of the National Suffrage Association opened in Washington on January 18, 1870. Among those chronicling the event was journalist Emily Edson Briggs, who wrote under the pseudonym Olivia. She described Stanton entering Lincoln Hall wearing black silk and a camel's hair scarf and, with her halo of white hair, looking "majestic and beautiful as a snowy landscape." Anthony, too, wore black silk with white lace gathered at her throat, "but even lace, frothy as sea-foam, failed to relieve that practical face." Anthony's visage was "hard, obdurate, uncompromising," like "a gnarled oak is among trees Susan B. Anthony is to her sex," Olivia observed. While sympathetic to "the cause," Oliva smarted at the way the conventioneers favored a competitor, the *New York Tribune,* over her newspaper, the *Press.* She noted that Anthony provided the *Tribune* reporter with insider papers and that the reporter, outfitted in a jaunty military suit trimmed with gilt cord and buttons "shows at once her determination to win a battle." The audience of mostly women was "not the curled, dainty fashionables of the capital" but a different breed, "sad-faced . . . sorrowful" women with few illusions about the long battle ahead.

Few members of Congress attended the convention, and the *Tribune* pronounced the session a failure in political persuasion. Still, it was a triumph of performance art. Olivia wrote that Stanton's familiar oratory "rises to the dignity of a great actress. The pauses, the gestures, one learns by heart. Do the great and good men of the world repeat themselves in the same way?" she wondered. Anthony called on the conventioneers to demand passage of a proposed Sixteenth Amendment, to grant women the vote. Her voice rising with indignation, she said there were black men so ignorant that when they went to the polls they expected to have a mule given them for their effort. "Vesuvius could be painted more easily than Susan at this supreme moment," Olivia wrote. On January 22, 1870, the final day of the convention, the women delegates gathered in the hearing room of the Senate Committee on the District of Columbia. They were there to persuade the committee to report out the bill to extend suffrage to women. Stanton spoke first. She argued eloquently that Congress should legislate for equality. But when she called on the male legislators for questions, an ominous silence followed. Anthony rose to face the congressional guns, a moment that Olivia captured with telling detail: "Lilac kid gloves covered her kind, strong hands and it was astonishing to us all to see how much she looked like a woman. She put her hands behind her as if it was best to have them in a safe place, and commenced by telling the gentlemen that they had it in their power to strike the word 'male' out of the Constitution. (Susan has a way of saying the word 'male' so that it sounds like the snapping of small arms.) In the District the experiment was tried of giving colored men their rights, and it seems as if this is a fitting place for the inauguration of a grander experiment—that of doing for the woman what you did for the Negro. It is only a long custom which you hate to break."

The gentlemen of Congress were unmoved. Judge Cook of Illinois, who chaired the House committee on the District, chided the women for wasting Congress's time. "There is too much to do here already," he said, insisting that Congress had "no time—absolutely no time" to consider such a measure. His sense of propriety had been offended, and reading about the episode, you can almost hear him clucking his displeasure. "At the same time he seemed to be looking for a hole to escape," Olivia wrote of the chairman's obvious discomfort. The session ended with the congressional lions slipping stealthily away, but not before Anthony buttonholed two or three. "'Sixteenth Amendment' was distilled from her lips like honey from flowers," Olivia observed. Senator Charles Sumner was there, "genial as a summer's sun." He had welcomed the petitions gathered by Anthony and Stanton when he was pushing through the Thirteenth Amendment. "Yet it was noticed that during the whole ordeal he never opened his lips, but endured all with the resignation of martyrdom. And thus the meeting of the Amazon warriors passed away." If Sumner, their best and perhaps only ally, would not act, what chance did the women have?

. . .

The following January, as the NSA's second convention got under way in Washington, the focus shifted from Stanton and Anthony to another female renegade: Victoria Woodhull. On her own and without any formal contact with the organized suffrage movement, Woodhull announced in April 1870 that she was a candidate for president. The NSA leaders admired her daring but did nothing to help her—nor did she ask for their support. The American Woman Suffrage Association openly disapproved. Woodhull refused to be discouraged, and tried to get Frederick Douglass to run with her for vice president. He refused to have anything to do with her and her Equal Rights Party, which he viewed as the figment of one woman's imagination and not a real party. Anthony was furious that Woodhull had used her name without permission. She worried that the party would divert money and attention away from the NSA, and expose the suffrage movement to ridicule if the party failed, which Anthony expected it would. She knew from decades of work how hard it was to build a viable organization.

A woman of great beauty and extraordinary boldness, Woodhull began life as a daughter of a traveling medicine man, where she learned the skills of a tent-show spiritualist and became adept at marketing anything, including herself. She careered through life, making fortunes and losing them, taking husbands and lovers and discarding them, defying tradition at every turn. She lived with the railroad tycoon Cornelius Vanderbilt, though she was married to somebody else, and there is no indication of a divorce. "Corneel" was a lonely widower who found solace in Woodhull and her equally flamboyant sister, Tennessee ("Tennie") Claflin. He happily bankrolled their ventures, including a first-ever brokerage firm headed by women where they proved deft investors in stocks and real estate. The duo was such an oddity that men would come and stare at them through the windows. To discourage the curiosity-seekers, the women posted a card that read: "All gentlemen will state their business and then retire at once." The sisters published a newspaper, *Woodhull & Claflin's Weekly*, which they used as a forum for feminist ideas and other unconventional thoughts, including the first English translation of the *Communist Manifesto*.

Her views could not have been more radical, yet Woodhull accomplished what her more straitlaced sisters could not. She had a coveted invitation to speak before the House Judiciary Committee, where she planned to make the case that women already had the right to vote under the Fourteenth Amendment. All Congress had to do was to pass enabling legislation known as a "declaratory act."

The Washington press previewed Woodhull's appearance, calling her "the New York sensation," and the suffragists interrupted their convention to go over and hear Woodhull. Given her flair for drama, everybody was expecting fireworks. The hearing room was packed. A newspaper article recounting the event noted that she is "no painted Jezebel" and wore an Alpine hat, which must have passed the normality test. Woodhull had dressed conservatively for the occasion in a dark dress that touched her shoetops, which was short for the times but still respectable. She proceeded to deliver in a clear, melodious voice a straightforward, well-argued case for woman suffrage. Since women were considered persons in their own right for the purpose of taxation, she saw no reason why Congress couldn't interpret the Fourteenth Amendment as covering women. If women can't vote, they're not people, and that's patently untrue, she declared.

Woodhull impressed her audience with her mastery of legal principles. Her presentation was like a legal brief, and no wonder, because a congressman from Massachusetts, Benjamin F. Butler, helped her with her remarks and probably wrote them for her. Butler is described as "a known admirer of Victoria," which meant that he was one of her lovers. Woodhull believed in what she called "free love," a phrase that most people, women and men, found unsettling because it meant overhauling divorce law and undermining the biblical view of marriage as sacred and everlasting. Woodhull was smart and well-versed on a range of issues and, in 1872, she became the first woman to run for president. Her platform is best remembered for advocating free love, which she viewed as the ultimate right for men and women. "I have an inalienable, constitutional and natural right to love whom I may love, to love as long, or as short a period as I can, to change that love every day if I please," she said.

Anthony was wary of this unbridled force of nature, but most of the suffragist leaders were enamored of the way Woodhull could command attention and of the burst of charisma she gave their long and dreary movement. The

House Judiciary Committee issued a report that Congress lacked the power to extend the Fourteenth Amendment to women. The gallant Butler issued a strongly worded minority report together with another congressman, from Iowa, but their words were just that: words. There would be no action. But when the NSA held its May 1872 meeting in Steinway Hall in New York, Woodhull and a contingent of her supporters were on hand, ready to dominate the proceedings. Anthony pointed out that the hall had been rented in her name expressly for a woman's convention, and proceeded to bar Woodhull. What unfolded was a clash of titans. As the second day's evening session drew to a close, Woodhull executed a surprise entrance through a side door and made her way to the stage, head held high in defiance. Anthony was ready. As Woodhull stepped to the platform, prepared to address the crowd, Anthony moved directly in front of her and ruled her out of order. Woodhull shouted out a motion to adjourn and to meet the next morning in nearby Apollo Hall to officially form the People's Party. Anthony loudly vetoed the motion, but to no avail. Woodhull continued to implore the audience. A desperate Anthony rushed backstage and ordered the janitor to turn out the gaslights.

The delegates made their way through the din and the darkness to the street. Stanton was humiliated. She accused Anthony of being narrow-minded and intolerant and said she would no longer serve as an officer of the NSA. Anthony was unanimously chosen president, but the fiasco left everybody feeling wounded and embarrassed. At the Apollo, Woodhull was chosen to lead the "National

Radical Reformers' Party," as it was finally named, with the goal of attaining human rights for humankind. Woman suffrage was but one of its planks, along with government-guaranteed employment for all, unlimited free speech, and a new federal Constitution. Woodhull was nominated to run for president. Frederick Douglass was nominated for vice president, but wasn't there and wouldn't have accepted anyway. "I nominate Spotted Tail," shouted out a delegate from the West. "An Injun is better than a nigger any day."

Woodhull's candidacy would go nowhere, and the accompanying scandal was said to set back the women's movement a decade. But when Woodhull made her splash, the drive for suffrage still had almost half a century to go before fruition. How could they tell?

Woodhull's character had come under severe attack by Henry Ward Beecher, an internationally celebrated clergyman who was the Billy Graham of his time. Beecher regularly assailed Woodhull and her sister as the worst purveyors of vice, a charge made possible by the double standard in vogue at the time. Women were the bearers of moral standards, and lapses were not tolerated. Men dominated the public sphere of life; personal misbehavior was overlooked and covered up. In public Woodhull was stoic and affected a brave manner, but in private she seethed at the pious Beecher, who, she knew, had carried on an affair some years earlier with one of his parishioners. The guilt-ridden woman had confessed the liaison to her husband, begging his forgiveness. But the husband, a well-known journalist named Theodore Tilton, had such trouble putting the episode behind him that his wife feared for her life.

The wife confided in Anthony, who confided in Stanton, who told Woodhull, and soon the story spun out of control. A few days before the November 1872 presidential election, Woodhull published the sordid details of the Beecher-Tilton affair in her newspaper. The account was so richly documented that Woodhull, in the finest journalistic tradition, must have had a second source. Speculation centered on the likelihood that she had gotten additional insider information after having an intimate relationship with the cuckolded husband. Woodhull wanted to bring down Beecher, a past president of the American Woman Suffrage Association, along with his pious admirers who acted so morally superior and had spurned Woodhull. She fancied herself striking a blow for women's rights in stripping away the veil of secrecy that surrounded Beecher's behavior. Her newspaper sold out in hours. People were so eager for the juicy details that some paid up to $40 for a single copy.

Americans were unaccustomed to sexual scandal spread across the pages of a newspaper, and the fact that women had brought these sordid details to light made it particularly shocking. Postal censor Anthony Comstock arrested Woodhull and Claflin for sending obscenity through the mail. The authorities held the sisters for seven months in a harsh prison known as the Tombs in New York City before releasing them. Their flirtation with the suffrage movement was over, but they went on to build new and successful lives in Europe, thanks to the financial largesse of the Vanderbilt family, who were willing to pay anything to get them out of the country. Both married again, and well, and continued to agitate for radical change until their deaths.

The other actors in the drama didn't fare as well. Theodore Tilton remained consumed with his wife's betrayal, and years after the affair had taken place, filed charges against Beecher for alienation of affection and adultery. The trial lasted six months and pitted the two suffrage associations against each other. The more conservative, American Woman Suffrage Association, stood by Beecher. He had been its first president, and his sister, the famed writer Harriet Beecher Stowe, was active in the group. Leaders of the NSA, including Beecher's half sister Isabella, made it clear they didn't believe his tortured version of events. Beecher spent more than $100,000 to defend himself. The all-male jury in the end could not reach a decision, and the case was dismissed. Public sympathy was with Beecher, and the sensational trial did not hurt his career as a celebrity preacher. Tilton went off to Europe to pout. It was Tilton's wife, Lib, the object of Beecher's affections, who bore the brunt of the negative publicity. She was excommunicated for her sins from the Brooklyn, New York, church, where Beecher remained as pastor. Lib Tilton lived in shame, without money or friends, nobody's hero in the sorry episode.

Anthony was pained by the whole experience, but determined to test Woodhull's thesis that the first sentence of the Fourteenth Amendment applied to women as well as the freed black population for whom it was intended. It said: "All persons born or naturalized in the United States and subject to the jurisdiction thereof, are citizens of the

United States and of the State wherein they reside." Citizens vote; ergo, women vote.

The election was looming, and on one of the last days for voter registration, Anthony and her two sisters, together with a dozen other women, arrived at the Rochester barbershop where the male registrars sat, and demanded that they be registered as voters. The men responded gently but firmly that the women must leave. Anthony read them the Fourteenth Amendment and said that if they forcibly ejected her and the other women, she would sue each one of them. The threat must have impressed the men—each young enough to be her sons, Anthony later noted— because they relented and added the women's names to the rolls. Inspired by Anthony's success, forty more women showed up the next day at the barbershop to register. On Election Day at seven in the morning, Anthony voted a straight Republican ticket.

Newspapers across the country carried front-page stories about Anthony's daring act, but the editorial pages were almost uniformly negative. Columnists and editorial writers screamed for her punishment. And there was no countervailing force. Women did not rise up in her defense; most women thought the vote unnecessary and a burden they did not wish to have. For more than three weeks after the election, the government did nothing. Then on Thanksgiving Day, a federal marshal arrived unannounced at the Anthony family home in Rochester with a warrant for Susan B. Anthony's arrest. She was fifty-two years old, and the marshal was clearly uncomfortable with the prospect of hauling off this woman to the district attorney's office. He told her that she should come by when it was convenient. "Oh, dear, no," said Anthony. "I much prefer to be taken, handcuffed if possible."

She wasn't about to let the government do this gracefully. If she were taken forcibly, she might win sympathy and front-page attention for the cause. She had the gentleman wait in the parlor while she went upstairs to change into a more pleasing outfit. When she was dressed and ready to go, she thrust out her wrists to be handcuffed. The marshal refused. Anthony said she wanted no special treatment. There were no police wagons in those days, so Anthony, in the company of her government captor, traveled downtown on a horse-drawn trolley. She made the most of the situation. When the conductor came to collect her fare, she refused him the nickel, proclaiming for all the passengers to hear, "I'm traveling at the expense of the federal government." Pointing to the embarrassed marshal, she said, "Ask him for my fare."

Anthony and her sisters and a dozen other women were formally arraigned in the same dreary room where fugitive slaves were once interrogated before being sent back to their masters. Bail was set at $500, which everyone but Anthony paid. Anthony applied for a writ of habeas corpus, which would allow her to present her case before the U.S. Supreme Court. When the judge refused the request and doubled her bail to $1,000, Anthony's lawyer, who was a family friend, took it upon himself to put up the money from his own funds. Only after they left the courthouse did Anthony realize that by paying the fine, she had forfeited her right to go to the U.S. Supreme Court. She confronted her lawyer. Did he realize he was ruining her constitutional case? "Yes," he replied, "but I could not see a lady I respected put in jail."

The resourceful Anthony still had some cards to play. As the lawyers discussed the trial date, she said she couldn't be tried until after December 10 because of her busy speaking schedule. The DA's jaw dropped, but he accommodated Anthony's request. The trial was set for the following June, time enough for her to visit all twenty-nine towns and villages in Monroe County, where she would be tried. Her new lecture was proving popular. Its title: "Is It a Crime for a Citizen of the United States to Vote?" At the end of each presentation, she would call for a show of hands. Every audience voted that it was not a crime, and pretty soon the authorities realized they could not find an unbiased jury in the Rochester area. Anthony had pulled off a public-relations coup. The prosecutor moved the trial to the circuit court in Canandaigua, the seat of neighboring Ontario County. Anthony took her lectures there and found many men willing to come forward and say they would acquit her.

As it turned out, no jury would get the chance to vote aye or nay. The trial was rigged from start to finish, presided over by Justice Ward Hunt, who wrote his opinion before the evidence was presented, and then ordered the jury to reach a guilty verdict. The case would never reach the U.S. Supreme Court, but it was as infamous a decision in 1873 for women as the Dred Scott decision of

1857 had been for slaves. In each case, the law was set aside to perpetuate deeply held biases with regard to the treatment of first blacks, and then women. Anthony was charged with fraudulent voting. If she had been acquitted, she would have walked out of the courtroom a free citizen able to vote in the next election, a result that Justice Hunt could not abide. He was new to his job; this was his first criminal case. His politically powerful mentor was the rabidly antisuffrage U.S. senator Roscoe Conkling, who was determined to squelch this voting fad before it got out of hand.

Hunt refused to let Anthony testify on her own behalf on the grounds that she, as a woman, was not competent. Her lawyer, Judge Henry Selden, took the unusual step of going into the witness box to testify that he had advised Anthony to vote, believing it was her right under the Fourteenth Amendment. Then, switching back from witness to lawyer, he delivered a three-hour presentation on the rights and privileges of citizenship. He concluded that if Anthony were to be condemned as a criminal for the noble act of voting, that condemnation "would only add another most weighty reason . . . to show that women need the aid of the ballot for their protection." As soon as the district attorney finished his summation, Hunt read the opinion he had drafted before even entering the chamber, which embraced a narrow view of the Fourteenth Amendment, and then he told the jury to find Anthony guilty.

Judge Selden rose to his feet to object that in a criminal case the judge can only charge the jury, and must allow it to reach its own verdict. Hunt didn't budge. Selden then demanded that Hunt poll the jury so the court could hear how each of the twelve men voted. Hunt refused, instead dismissing the jury, several of whom said outside the court that they would have voted in Anthony's favor. When the court convened the next day for sentencing, Selden requested a new trial, which Hunt, of course, denied. He ordered Anthony to stand, and then he uttered a line he would soon regret: "Has the prisoner anything to say why sentence shall not be pronounced?"

"Yes, Your Honor, I have many things to say," Anthony began. And the words tumbled out in a torrent. Her natural rights, her civil rights, her political rights, and her judicial rights—every vital principle of a democratic government—had been ignored. She had been degraded from the status of a citizen to that of a subject. "A commoner of England, tried before a jury of lords, would have far less cause to complain than I, a woman, tried before a jury of men." For the first time in the proceedings, the judge was not in control, and he wasn't happy about it. He tried half a dozen times to cut short Anthony's impassioned speech, but she would have none of it. She was polite, sometimes exaggeratedly so, calling Hunt "Your Honor," but she would not stop talking. She believed that it was wrong to treat her as a lawbreaker, just as it was wrong to punish those who helped free slaves when it was against the law.

"But yesterday, the same man-made forms of law declared it a crime punishable with $1,000 fine and six months' imprisonment to give a cup of cold water, a crust of bread, or a night's shelter to a panting fugitive tracking his way to Canada; and every man or woman in whose veins coursed a drop of human sympathy violated that wicked law, reckless of consequences, and was justified in so doing," she said. "And then the slaves who got their freedom had to take it over or under or through the unjust forms of law, precisely as now must women take it to get their right to a voice in this government; and I have taken mine, and mean to take it at every opportunity."

At the close of her speech, Anthony told the judge she wanted no lenience from him, and wished her sentence to reflect "the full rigor of the law." Judge Hunt, annoyed and flustered, ordered her to pay a fine of $100 and to cover the costs of the prosecution. "I will never pay a dollar of your unjust penalty," she said. She never did, and the government didn't try to collect.

The trial generated a wave of sympathy for Anthony and the suffrage movement. "If it is a mere question of who has got the best of it, Miss Anthony is still ahead," opined one upstate New York newspaper. "She has voted and the American Constitution has survived the shock. Fining her one hundred dollars does not rule out the fact that . . . women voted, and went home, and the world jogged on as before."

Newspaper editorials everywhere saw the trial as a travesty of justice. Never before had any white person been refused the right to testify in his or her own behalf, or denied a jury trial. For the first time, Anthony's gender was a secondary matter to her rights as an American citizen. The *New York Sun* called for Judge Hunt's impeachment, and many other newspapers, even those opposed to woman suffrage, joined in skewering Hunt. Editorial writers pointed out that Hunt's calumny extended to his refusal to give Anthony a choice between a fine and serving time. Had she chosen prison, she could have appealed her case to a higher court and perhaps gotten a different verdict.

The three election registrars who had accepted the ballots of Anthony and fourteen other women in the eighth ward of Rochester were each fined $25 plus the cost of their prosecution. They refused to pay and were sent to prison, where a contingent of Rochester women brought them delicious, home-cooked meals each day. After a week, President Ulysses Grant pardoned the three men.

Anthony's lawyer took the unusual step of appealing to Congress, asking the Senate and House Judiciary Committees to uphold the right of trial by jury and to overturn Anthony's fine. Both committees declined to get involved. "Congress cannot be converted into a national court of review for any and all criminal convictions where it shall be alleged that the judge has committed an error," said a House report. Any official acknowledgment that Judge Hunt had acted illegally could have sparked a nationwide rush by women to the ballot box. As it was, Anthony had three thousand copies of the court transcript of her exchange with Hunt printed and distributed to activists around the country. She couldn't have had a better calling card to spur like-minded women to action.

Anthony was not alone in her attempt to vote in 1872, though she was the most notorious. Some 150 women across the country confronted their local officials to test this right of their citizenship. One of them, Virginia

Minor of St. Louis, a former president of the Missouri Woman Suffrage Association, decided to sue when she was turned away. Luckily, she was married to an attorney who was willing to spend two years of his time arguing her case against a St. Louis election official. *Minor* v. *Happersett* went all the way to the U.S. Supreme Court, where a decision handed down in October 1874 said that only the states had the right to grant suffrage, and that the Fourteenth and Fifteenth Amendments banned discrimination based on race but not on sex. The ruling echoed the Court's infamous Dred Scott decision, where the justices had ruled the plaintiff was less than a human being because of race. Now the Court had ruled that women, because of sex, were less than human.

The courts were a dead end, which left women with two courses of action, each equally daunting. They could conduct state-by-state campaigns and win the vote one state at a time, or they could go to the heart of the problem and lobby Congress to amend the Constitution. Anthony was too impatient for the state-by-state strategy, though she would eventually reconcile herself to its necessity, if only as a matter of leverage. She hadn't given up on Washington.

It was another national election year, 1876, and Democrat Samuel J. Tilden of New York was running against Republican Rutherford B. Hayes of Ohio. Both were governors, and neither was particularly distinguished. Anthony hoped to introduce a wedge issue into the campaign with petitions for an amendment. She had ten thousand names on petitions from twenty-six states, and without the proper escort, she crashed the House chamber to hand the petitions to the congressmen from those states. The multivolume *History of Woman Suffrage,* written by the leaders and edited by Ida Husted Harper, noted that Anthony, "on finding herself suddenly whisked into those sacred enclosures, amid a crowd of stalwart men, spittoons and scrap baskets," felt so out of place as a woman that she laughingly apologized to one of her congressional allies. He took it in good graces, telling her, "I hope yet to see you on this floor, in your own right, and in business hours, too." Anthony carried her petitions onto the Senate floor as well, where she was treated courteously. The men knew better than to create a confrontation that would only help Anthony. But they made sure that her petitions had no impact, referring them to the Committee on Public Lands, where they would gather dust.

4

Passing the Torch

The climate for women was improving. Anthony joined Stanton on the speech circuit, and together they were tireless as they crisscrossed the country. Travel was laborious in those days. The women would leave home in October or November, each with a huge trunk of clothes, and stay on the road until spring, usually in the Midwest, but sometimes all the way to the Pacific Coast. For weeks at a time, they spoke each night and traveled all day. A postwar boom in railroad construction made the travel possible, but it was not easy. Incomplete rail lines required stagecoaches, boats, and sleighs as backup. Anthony documented a few December days in Wisconsin in 1877 as a typical experience: After speaking in Milwaukee on Sunday afternoon, she took a midnight train to Green Bay, where she spoke on Monday, and traveled six hours by train and stagecoach on Tuesday to lecture at Stevens Point. On Wednesday she wrote: "Left [Stevens] Point at 8 A.M.—carriage to Pover—mud and slush—five miles—then freight to New London—and then freight to Appleton arriving 4 P.M.—and lo my trunk had been set off at Hortonville—so I had to get my beefsteak—got to bed—but couldn't sleep—and go to Platform in my travelling gear—was introduced by Prof. Sawyer—of the Lawrence University here—had splendid audience but didn't feel at home in my mohair gray travelling dress." Despite a cold that reached "the sneezing stage" and roads of "mud without precedent," she kept up this pace.

In the years since the Civil War, state campaigns for woman suffrage had sprung up in Ohio, Michigan, Missouri, Kansas, Wisconsin, Minnesota, and Wyoming, and the list continued to grow. Anthony and Stanton were important figures around the country, rallying women and popularizing suffrage beyond any organized movement. Anthony was invited to address state legislatures where suffrage measures were being debated, a reflection of the growing stature of the movement. Beginning in 1866, delegations of women from around the country presented every session of Congress with petitions demanding the vote. Finally, on January 10, 1878, California senator Aaron A. Sargent introduced a Sixteenth Amendment, as drafted by Stanton and Anthony. It said simply: "The right of citizens to vote shall not be denied or abridged by the United States or by any State on account of sex." Known as the "Susan B. Anthony Amendment," it made the front page of the *New York Tribune,* not a long story but "a biting and scathing one," according to a 1919 retrospective piece in the newspaper. "It portrayed women as invading the Senate and having the impertinence to buttonhole the senators on their way to lunch in a way that made them uncomfortable."

Stanton had the task of testifying before the Senate Committee on Privileges and Elections, and the lawmakers let her know how they felt through their body language. "I never felt more exasperated standing before a committee of men many years my junior, all comfortably seated in armchairs," she wrote of the experience. "Particularly aggravating" was the "studied inattention and contempt" of the chairman, Senator Benjamin Wadleigh of New Hampshire. A portly gentleman with muttonchop whiskers, he stretched, yawned, gazed at the ceiling, sharpened his pencil, rifled through a newspaper, even cut his nails as she spoke. "It was with difficulty that I restrained the impulse . . . to hurl my manuscript at his head," she said. The amendment did not make it out of committee that year and had to be reintroduced in each session of Congress for the next forty-two years.

Antisuffragists also testified before Congress. They were fewer in number, but they were well connected. The wives of two popular Civil War commanders, Mrs. William Sherman and Mrs. James Dahlgren, founded the Woman's Anti-Suffrage Association of Washington City. Dahlgren's husband had been a navy admiral, and she had no trouble getting a hearing on Capitol Hill whenever she wanted. In 1878 she testified in opposition to the newly proposed Sixteenth Amendment. Her objections were familiar: Marriage is a sacred unity; there is only one head of a household. If women gain the vote, it upsets the natural order and sows "division and discord" in the family unit and in the country.

.   .   .

Suffrage had gained respectability, but it did not inspire passion. Politicians could ignore the countless petitions filed with Congress without fear that women would rise and demand their rights. Women were still ambivalent about whether they wanted the vote. Another cause spoke to women in a way that suffrage never had, and that was the temperance movement. The Women's Christian Temperance Union (WCTU) was formally established in 1874 after women in Ohio and western New York marched on saloons and held vigils, singing and praying, until the saloonkeepers shut their doors in self-defense. It was a temporary victory, since most soon reopened, but a powerful political movement was under way. Women blamed much of society's ills on men's easy access to drink. Prostitution was growing, and one in ten men had syphilis, which they would bring home to their wives. Dr. Elizabeth Blackwell, the first woman to receive a medical degree in the United States, called it "family plus prostitution." Under the leadership of Frances Willard, the group's visionary president, the WCTU had 150,000 dues-paying members, a hundred times more members than the suffragists could claim. Willard was pious, puritanical, and intensely political. She said that while praying she had heard from God, who told her "to speak for woman's ballot as a weapon of protection to her home . . . from the tyranny of drink." Among the WCTU's ardent supporters was Lucy Hayes, wife of President Rutherford B. Hayes. Lucy banned drinking in the White House and was known as "Lemonade Lucy." Bars sprang up near the White House with names such as "Last Chance," in a mocking response to the first lady's dictum. Though the WCTU favored suffrage, Lucy remained studiously neutral on the subject. She turned down an invitation to give the commencement speech at a women's medical college for fear it might be interpreted as favoring feminist aspirations, though she did visit the college in a quiet show of support.

Anthony was traveling with an almost manic intensity during this period. She would go anywhere and speak to anybody who would have her. She went into saloons to beseech the customers; she spoke to inmates at a local insane asylum. She reached out to the wives of Mormon elders, the Daughters of the American Revolution, and the National Association of Colonial Women. During the last quarter of the nineteenth century, women had created a wide array of their own groups to serve as social networks and provide an entrée into politics. Anthony envisioned uniting all these diverse women's groups around the goal of the vote. She didn't care what other positions they held. She wanted to build a coalition that could make an impression in Washington.

When Willard created a separate department within the WCTU to press for suffrage, Anthony embraced her as a valuable ally. Willard could marshal tens of thousands of women for suffrage. The two women were alike. Both were former teachers, unmarried, who had dedicated their lives to reforming the world around them. But it was hard to separate suffrage from the WCTU's other goals, most of which were conservative, religiously oriented, and at odds with the suffrage movement's more liberal attitudes. The WCTU was lobbying Congress to declare Christianity America's official faith; they wanted Sunday blue laws strictly enforced and extended to baseball stadiums and amusement parks; and they wanted religious instruction in public schools. Many leading suffragists regarded Willard as a dangerous figure, and openly rebuked Anthony for her naïveté in seeing Willard as an ally. Most WCTU members had no interest in women's rights. Anthony said she didn't mind individuals agitating for laws against cigarettes, gambling, and racing, whatever they deemed immoral, but she didn't want to give these activities the blessing of the suffrage movement. And while she herself abstained from alcohol and was once active in the temperance movement, she refused to endorse prohibition.

It was a losing battle. Just as the white ribbons WCTU members wore to symbolize the purity of the "true woman" were now intertwined with yellow, the color of suffrage, the two causes had become one and the same in the public mind. The conflict came to a head in California, where state suffrage was on the ballot in 1896, and the suffragists working the campaign worried that the WCTU's heavy moralizing would turn off male voters. "What I want is for the men to vote 'yes' on the suffrage amendment, and I don't ask whether they make wine on the ranches or believe that Christ made it at the wedding feast," Anthony wrote to Stanton. Anthony convinced Willard to move a planned WCTU convention in San Francisco to St. Louis, and to stay out of the California fight. But the prohibition forces were too plentiful and powerful to cease and desist. They let it be known that if the amendment passed, they would be back in the state to destroy the winemaking and distillery industries, a major part of the California economy. The vineyard owners struck back, and support for the amendment dropped precipitously as the state's major newspapers opposed the suffrage measure, citing the potential economic damage.

The amendment lost, and the WCTU women blamed the evil saloon conspiracy. Anthony knew better; it was their own political ignorance that had cost them the victory. She wrote to Willard in frustration: "Don't you see, if women ever get the right to vote, it must be through the consent of not only the moral and decent men of the nation, but also through that of the other kind? Is it not perfectly idiotic of us to be telling the latter class that the first thing we shall do with our ballots will be to knock them out of their pet pleasures and vices? If you still think it wise to keep on sticking pins into the men you will have to go on doing it. I certainly shall not be one of your helpers in that particular line of work." Despite her outburst, Anthony remained in awe of Willard and the extraordinary charisma she brought to an otherwise dour movement. When Willard died at age fifty-eight in 1898, Anthony said, "I never approached her but what I felt my nerves tingle from this magnetism."

By the late 1880s, the suffrage movement was stalled. Efforts to pass a constitutional amendment were going nowhere. In an 1887 Senate vote, the measure was defeated, thirty-four to sixteen. It was seen as so trivial and politically unimportant that twenty-five senators didn't even bother to show up for the vote. The emphasis on state campaigning wasn't bearing fruit either. Women had won the vote in a handful of school board and city elections, but by 1887 just two territories—Utah and Wyoming—had fully enfranchised women. Each acted in unique self-interest. Utah had been ostracized because of its support for polygamy, and suffrage was its way of proving respect for women. In 1869 Wyoming Territory extended suffrage before it achieved statehood as a way of attracting more families and women to settle in the sparsely populated area. Neither territory could be held up as a victory for the suffrage movement.

After eleven years on the road, Stanton thought it was time to take stock. She had tired of the accolades, and questioned whether all the travel made any difference. It was March 1879, and she was counting the days until her lecture tour would end. She felt "like a squeezed sponge" with nothing left to share. It was time to regenerate, and Stanton returned home to Tenafly, New Jersey, where she determined to write a history of the movement that had consumed so much of her life. Anthony joined her in the project together with an old friend, Matilda Jocelyn Gage, a thoughtful intellectual who proved the movement's most reliable historian. The daughter of a physician and the wife of a wealthy merchant, Gage brought balance to the volatile Stanton-Anthony collaboration. The project took six years, produced nearly six thousand pages, and strained each woman's patience. "I'd rather make history than write it," Anthony complained. But the friendships endured, along with the first three volumes of the *History of Woman Suffrage,* a thorough if sometimes tedious account of the early struggle.

Anthony felt the breath of time on her back. She'd always been a person of narrow focus, but now she wanted to shut out every distraction that could hurt the cause of suffrage. When word arrived in 1884 that Frederick Douglass had married a white woman named Helen Pitts, many of Douglass's friends and admirers were openly dismayed. His first wife, Anna, was a freedwoman who had given him all her savings so he could escape bondage and flee to Massachusetts. She never learned to read, but stayed home to tend their children and help Douglass publish his newspaper. Anna had recently died after a long illness. Douglass's name was still prominent in suffrage circles, and his remarriage inevitably turned attention to the blending of the races, an emotional subject that critics could then use to tar the movement. Stanton, always more open to radical views about marriage and race, dispatched a warm note of congratulations to Douglass. She urged Anthony to do the same, and even drafted a letter for both of them to sign, wishing Douglass well and inviting him to speak at their next convention. Anthony refused to add her name, and instead dispatched this curt letter to Stanton, who was in England:

I do hope you won't put your foot into the question of intermarriage of the races. It has no place on our platform, any more than the question of no marriage at all, or of polygamy and, so far as I can prevent it, shall not be brought there. I beg you therefore not to congratulate him publicly. Our intention at this convention is to make every one who hears or reads believe in the grand principle of equality of rights and chances for women, and if they see on our program the name of Douglass every thought will be turned toward the subject of amalgamation and away from that of woman and her disfranchised. . . . Do not throw around that marriage the halo of a pure and lofty duty to break down race lines. Your sympathy has run away with your judgment.

Anthony continued to admire Douglass, but she never softened her stand on his marriage, or altered her belief that the race issue was a distraction. She personally persuaded Douglass not to attend a suffrage convention in Atlanta for fear that his presence would undermine her effort to recruit white Southerners. After Reconstruction, southern states systematically imposed laws to deny the vote to black men, and they had no interest in opening up votes for black women. While Anthony's private views were unchanged—she believed in equality between the races—she concluded it was now the woman's hour, and the black man would have to wait.

Younger women had little knowledge of and no first-hand participation in the bitter debate over race and tactics that had split the movement in 1869. Neither organization—the NSA or the AWSA—could claim success, and it seemed silly to maintain two separate groups of aging leaders when the younger generation had no memory of what divided them in the first place. One of Lucy Stone's daughters initiated talks with Anthony about merging into a single organization dedicated solely to gaining the vote. All other issues would be submerged. Anthony was initially wary, and it took more than two years for Alice Stone Blackwell to cement the deal, in February 1890. By then her mother was ill and unable to propose herself as a possible first president for the newly combined National American Woman Suffrage Association (NAWSA). That left Stanton or Anthony as the most obvious choice.

Anthony could not bear to run against the woman who had been her friend and mentor and who had introduced her to the movement. She beseeched the delegates to vote for Stanton, and they obliged, installing Stanton as the NAWSA's first president, with Anthony vice president. Lucy Stone agreed to chair the executive committee. Stanton planned to return to England the next day, and her inaugural address had the tone of a valedictory. Seemingly oblivious to the delicate diplomacy that set the stage for the merger, Stanton said, "We do not want to limit our platform to bare suffrage and nothing more. . . . Wherever a woman is wronged her voice should be heard." She had misgivings about the new organization and its direction. "I get more radical as I get older, where Susan seems to grow more conservative," she fretted. Two years later she turned the NAWSA presidency over to Anthony.

Stanton was traveling when she received a cablegram
that her husband was dead of pneumonia. They had been
apart for much of their forty-six-year union. She sold the
home they shared in Tenafly, New Jersey, and never committed herself to another permanent household, preferring
to move about and stay with children and friends. When in
1888 Anthony decided to commemorate the fortieth
anniversary of the convention at Seneca Falls, Stanton was
in London, and after initially promising to attend, she concluded it was too much of an effort. Dreading yet another
lengthy ocean crossing, she wrote Anthony to carry on
without her. Anthony was white hot with anger. She
waited a day and a night before replying, then penned a
letter that conveyed her feelings in such strong terms that
she wrote in her diary, "It will start every white hair in her
head." Ten days later, a cable arrived from Stanton with
just three words: "I am coming."

Anthony was ecstatic. Stanton's speech, she knew,
would be the centerpiece of the celebration. For once, she
wouldn't want Stanton muzzled. This was an occasion for
passion and big ideas and a vision for the coming century.
But when Stanton arrived, she had no speech. Just getting
herself across the Atlantic was arduous enough. She
weighed more than 240 pounds and had difficulty getting
around in the ship's tight quarters. Anthony was devas-
tated but not defeated. She put Stanton under virtual
house arrest, shutting her up in a hotel room at the Riggs
House in Washington, D.C., with a guard posted at the
door. Her every need would be taken care of, but Anthony
made it clear: Stanton would not leave the room until she

had a speech in hand. Stanton made light of the situation. "Although most women are under the thumb of a man, I prefer a tyrant of my own sex," she said.

The aging giants of the suffrage movement stood together for the last time at the fortieth anniversary of the convention at Seneca Falls, their differences forgotten, their struggle still unresolved. Among them was Frederick Douglass, whose stately presence spoke to his unshaken support for suffrage despite the exclusions dealt him in the name of political expediency. It was a grand moment, followed by a reception at the White House hosted by the first lady, Frances Folsom Cleveland. Only twenty-one years old when she married Grover Cleveland, a middle-aged bachelor more than twice her age, Frances was the Jackie Kennedy of her day. Her youth and beauty captivated the public, and she could start a trend simply by changing her hairstyle. But she was more than a stylish ornament as first lady. A college graduate, she sympathized with efforts to better the lives of women, pointedly holding receptions on Saturday afternoons so ordinary women—seamstresses, teachers, and factory workers—could attend. So many people clamored to meet her that after standing for hours shaking hands, she would have her arms wrapped in ice to ease the aching. Though she supported the WCTU, she didn't like the moralizing and rebuffed the temperance women's request that she stop wearing low-cut dresses. She never took a stand on suffrage; neither did she disavow the cause, leaving it to the public's imagination when she invited suffrage leaders to the White House.

From the number of teas, dinners, and receptions held in their honor by senators and other important people, you would think success was at hand. But victory was still thirty-two years away, and none of the leaders present that glorious day would live to see the moment of victory.

A rare breakthrough occurred when the men of Colorado voted in 1893 to give women full voting rights, only the second state to do so (after Wyoming, which became a state in 1890). The successful campaign brought to light the talents of Carrie Chapman Catt, who would soon emerge to lead the suffrage movement for the next thirty years. Graduating first in her class at Iowa State Agricultural College, she had become a school superintendent in just three years. Iowa was still the frontier, and women were scarce, so there was more opportunity, a lesson that made Catt more respectful of frontier society and its rough-hewn ways than her eastern compatriots. Her first husband, journalist Leo Chapman, died shortly after they married, and she remarried, in 1890, to George Catt, who signed a prenuptial agreement allowing her to spend four months of every year traveling to promote suffrage. She had the sensibility of a frontier woman and the fiber that comes with a life of hardship. She was a relentless organizer and willing to endure all manner of physical discomfort. Campaigning in South Dakota, she caught typhoid and almost died. She didn't have any of the effete ways of the eastern suffragists, most of whom came from upper-class backgrounds and looked down on frontier men as lowlifes. The secret to her success in Colorado was her absolute refusal to allow the WCTU to play a role, knowing that their excessive displays of virtue would create a backlash against suffrage.

The old warhorses were dying off, and their passing exposed some ugly truths. Sojourner Truth, the charismatic former slave who had electrified so many suffrage conventions, died in 1883 and was buried in Battle Creek, Michigan, where she had finally settled after years of continuous travel. She was able to live off the proceeds of her memoir, which she had dictated to a white woman, since Truth had never learned to read or write. Truth died a hero to the suffrage movement, but when the NAWSA convened its convention in Michigan in 1899, it was not to honor her. The stain of racism had spread to the suffrage movement. Suffagists who had been ardent abolitionists now wanted nothing to do with the mounting oppression of the South's black citizens. Segregation was replacing slavery. Frederick Douglass, the last conscience of the movement on race issues, died in 1895 at age seventy-seven. He was on his way home from a suffrage rally when he was stricken by a massive heart attack.

Elizabeth Cady Stanton made her last voyage across the ocean in 1892, returning to the States. She was so grossly overweight and hobbled by deteriorating eyesight that a paid companion was engaged to help her get around. Anthony was both moved and disgusted by Stanton's condition. In the blunt language that characterized their relationship, Anthony urged Stanton to settle on a place "you can call your own so you can cremate yourself in your own oven should you desire." Anthony had moved back to her family home in Rochester and was living with her sister Mary. Stanton could join them, Anthony offered. But Stanton declined, moving into the Manhattan apartment of her daughter and son-in-law, irking Anthony once more.

At the 1900 convention, everybody expected Anthony to turn over the presidency to the Reverend Anna Shaw, a Methodist preacher known for her ability to deliver stem-winding sermons. If she'd been a man, everybody agreed, she would have been recruited by a big urban church a long time ago. Anthony was drawn to her for the same reason she bonded with Stanton. Shaw was a wordsmith, and a merry soul as well, like Stanton roly-poly in appearance and at home in the spotlight. So it was a shock to NAWSA when instead of Shaw, Anthony turned instead to Catt, a woman more like herself, a tactician and an organizer. Catt couldn't inspire a crowd in a convention hall the way Shaw could, but she knew how to win elections. Fifty-two years of speeches hadn't gained suffrage. Anthony instinctively knew that the final push had to be more than talk. Catt had followed up the Colorado victory that initially brought her to Anthony's notice with a successful referendum drive in Idaho. By 1896, women had the vote in four western states—Wyoming, Utah, Colorado, and Idaho. Catt was two for two, an impressive record in a movement that had experienced such a string of losses. But the promise of Catt was cut short when her husband fell ill, and she resigned the presidency in 1904 to care for him. Shaw stepped into the breach, and headed the organization with great flourish but few tangible results until 1914.

From today's perspective, it is outrageous that women didn't have their most fundamental rights. But most women until the turn of the twentieth century did not want the vote. It wasn't until the Industrial Revolution—which took hold in the United States largely after the Civil War—that women began to see the benefit of engaging in public life. With machines to free them from the drudgery of household chores, women could imagine a life beyond the confines of the home. But the suffrage movement by this point was such a fixture on the American scene that it lacked revolutionary fervor. Anthony was a familiar figure at Republican and Democratic conventions, and she was routinely welcomed at the White House by each succeeding president, and treated like a visiting dignitary. President McKinley, elected in 1896 and reelected in 1900, even took her into the family's private quarters to meet with his invalid wife, Ida, who later sent her a pair of bedroom slippers she had knitted. Historians are divided about whether Ida McKinley was truly ill or in the grip of neuroses. She was so fearful for her husband's safety that she rarely left her bed, pleading illness and thus insuring he didn't venture far from her side. Although the Civil War had ended more than twenty years earlier, Ida continued to knit slippers for the soldiers—blue for Union troops, gray for the Confederacy, and bright colors for orphaned children—producing literally thousands of slippers during her time in the White House. Why she undertook this questionable task was anybody's guess.

.   .   .

While suffrage languished, the prohibitionist movement was gaining momentum. Carry Nation, a poor Kansas woman who blamed male alcoholism for everything that had gone wrong in her life, resorted to violence to make her point. She hurled rocks and bottles at saloons, and even armed herself with a hatchet, which became her symbol. She was arrested repeatedly, but her support grew with each offense as her followers sang and prayed outside of whatever jail she was held in. The WCTU initially condoned her behavior, pointing out that the saloons she attacked were operating in areas that were supposed to be dry. But when Nation began selling hatchets at a Coney Island carnival, they ousted her from their organization. Nation also made the suffragists squirm because she exposed an uncomfortable truth about the woman's vote and its inability to make a practical difference. Women had been voting in local school elections in Kansas since 1861, and in 1887, Kansas extended the vote to municipal elections, adding thousands of women to the rolls and legalizing prohibition. But the politicians protected the liquor sellers, and the state was as wet as ever. When Nation applied her hatchet to the politicians' favorite hangout, she was run out of town and left to wander the country for targets of opportunity. In 1910 she met her match in a female bar owner in Montana, who beat Nation so senseless she died six months later.

Watching from afar, Stanton was perhaps the only suffrage leader to openly cheer Nation's militancy when she first started smashing Kansas saloons. "I wish we had ten thousand 'Madame Nations,' smashing the gilded mirrors and ornaments in the haunts of vice in every state of the Union," Stanton wrote in 1901, when Nation was just getting under way. Anthony disapproved, of course, but held her tongue publicly and privately, too, refusing to break with her old friend. In June 1902, Anthony stopped by the Manhattan apartment where Stanton was living, immobilized by weight and age, and virtually blind. "Shall I see you again?" Anthony asked as she was leaving, fearing this would be their last meeting. "Oh, yes," Stanton replied in her usual jaunty manner, "if not here, then in the hereafter, if there is one—and if there isn't, we shall never know it." Stanton died four months later, on October 26, 1902. She left instructions about her dress—"no crepe or black, no fripperies or fandangos"—and asked that "some common sense women" conduct the funeral services. The mahogany table on which she drafted the Declaration of Sentiments fifty years earlier at Seneca Falls was placed at the head of her casket. A framed photograph of Anthony stood atop the casket, reflecting the new reality and prompting the headline "Stanton Dead; Anthony Left Behind."

The premonition that haunted Ida McKinley came true on a September day in 1901 during a visit to Buffalo, New York, when a self-professed anarchist, Leon Czolgosz, approached the president. He was clean-shaven and well dressed, and the handkerchief covering his right arm and hand apparently did not arouse suspicion. As McKinley reached to shake the man's left hand, Czolgosz pumped two bullets into the president from a pistol concealed beneath the white cloth. McKinley died from infection caused by his wounds a week later, elevating his vice president, Teddy Roosevelt, to the presidency. Americans were already paranoid about the potential dangers posed by foreigners. After McKinley's death at the hand of a foreign-born anarchist, suffragists found a receptive audience for their argument that the votes of educated white women would keep the society from being overrun by foreign elements.

For whatever reason, political or personal, Roosevelt stayed silent on suffrage, though he sometimes taunted the true believers. He liked to say a wife is equal, but her place should be in the home. He once said a woman is actually a criminal if she doesn't stay home with her twelve children. When asked about the statement, he replied, "I said four children, not twelve." Yet he treated Anthony with enormous respect and even warmth, greeting her like a friend, and toward the end of her life, inviting her to the White House for a private interview on the suffrage issue.

Anthony knew the 1906 NAWSA convention in Baltimore would be her last. It was snowing and cold, and after attending an opening dinner, she was too weak to make it to any of the sessions. Upon learning that two women of great wealth whom she had personally recruited had pledged $60,000 to continue NAWSA's work, Anthony pronounced herself well enough to attend a dinner in Washington to mark her eighty-sixth birthday. Among the tributes was a letter from President Roosevelt. Hearing Roosevelt's glowing words, Anthony rose and despite her

weakened state mustered some of her old fire.
from President Roosevelt in his [State of the
message would be worth a thousand eulogies to Su
Anthony. When will men learn that what we ask is
praise, but justice?" Anthony rallied enough to deliver to
the Baltimore convention what would be her final speech
and the most memorable words of her long crusade,
"Failure is impossible." She returned home to Rochester,
New York, where she died a month later, on March 14,
1906. The day of her funeral was bitter cold with a driving
snow, yet ten thousand people stood outside the church,
waiting to pay their respects. Anthony was dressed in her
familiar black with a lace collar set off by a pin given to her
by the women of Wyoming for her eightieth birthday. A
jeweled flag with a diamond represented each of the suffrage states. The pin was removed just before the casket
was closed and given to Anna Shaw, Anthony's successor
and loyal companion.

Hundreds of newspaper columns were devoted to
Anthony's passing and the mark she had made on American history, but the inevitability of woman suffrage was not
yet wholly obvious. "She was the champion of a lost
cause," declared one editorial writer. "Her peculiar views
on this question will soon be forgotten," asserted another.
There was a school of thought that without Anthony's
activism and inspiration, the woman's movement would
fade away. As one editor put it, "There is reason for the
belief that it will gradually subside."

"One word
Union]
an B.
ot

5

Division in the Ranks

Movements ebb and flow, their contours change, and people are at odds over strategy and tactics, but never the goal, so they move in the same direction, however slowly or fitfully. After Anthony's passing, the suffrage movement split between the moderates and the radicals. The head moderate was Carrie Chapman Catt, who drew up what she called the "Winning Plan." It focused on winning suffrage state by state, and putting in place the machinery to lobby lawmakers and influence voters. Her *Organizing to Win* pamphlet took women through the mundane process of creating a political operation, from naming precinct captains to distributing suffrage propaganda. Eleanor Roosevelt called Catt the most organized woman she knew, and the American woman she admired most. Like Anthony, in whose footsteps she followed, Catt was a tactician, daunting in her ability to coordinate chapters all around the country. The NAWSA under Catt became the League of Women Voters, known today as it was then for its issue-based, bipartisan approach to politics and its aversion to protests or flashy displays of any kind.

The head radical was Alice Paul, who lived to create a stir and whose outrage fueled demonstrations designed to embarrass and anger the Democrats in power for opposing suffrage. Paul was a generation younger than Catt, and Paul brimmed with an impatience that sprang from her conviction that she had the answer. Born a Quaker in 1885, she showed no early inclination toward feminism. Her letters home as a schoolgirl were filled with references to "Thee" and "Thou," reflecting her strict Quaker beginnings. These letters are not introspective; they tend to be practical, a mirror image of her personality. Paul had an extraordinary degree of education for a woman of the time—indeed, of any time. She had a bachelor's degree from Swarthmore and a master's degree and a Ph.D. from the University of Pennsylvania. She also was a graduate of the New York School of Philanthropy, and in 1907 headed for England as a graduate student to study social work, which was an avant-garde subject for women.

Upper-class women went to college abroad in the early part of the twentieth century much as they do today. Paul traveled first to Germany and then to England, which was the center of the world intellectually and where all the new social work theories were being developed. Working in the London slums, Paul happened upon a street-corner speech on women's rights. She was captivated, and soon became an acolyte of a radicalized upper-middle-class woman named Mrs. Emmeline Pankhurst, who, with her two daughters acting as lieutenants, was at the forefront of

Britain's militant suffrage movement. Pankhurst had turned to street protests after having her ideas dismissed at local council meetings. She was convinced that only the vote could confer respect. There was nothing polite about the Pankhursts. They thumbed their noses at the law, chalking sidewalks with notices of their meetings and parading through the streets with a hurdy-gurdy and a monkey. They encouraged their followers to crash government meetings and harass public officials, and when arrested, to go on hunger strikes, all in the service of gaining publicity for their cause. Paul immediately fell in with the Pankhursts, and it wasn't long before she was arrested and jailed for disrupting Parliament. Detained in the billiard room of a local police station, the only area large enough to hold more than a hundred protesters, Paul noticed a woman her age wearing a small American flag. Lucy Burns, a graduate of Vassar on a holiday break from her studies, had gotten swept up in the movement just like Paul.

The two women became fast friends and were twice arrested together, staging hunger strikes to attract attention and to provoke their jailers into releasing them early. But the prison authorities were on to the Pankhursts and their tactics. The next time Paul was arrested and sentenced along with another protester to thirty days in jail, refusing to eat did not win her freedom. Instead, the authorities forcibly fed the women, a painful procedure that involved inserting a tube down the throat and pouring in liquid food. Paul's mother was desperate for information about her daughter, and sent a letter to the U.S. ambassador in England, seeking his help. The response she received was officious and not in the least sympathetic. Militant suffragists were not high on his list. The experience took its toll on Paul's health, and she was pale and emaciated when she recovered enough to set sail for America in January 1910.

Paul arrived in time to attend her first convention of the NAWSA, which turned out to be an exercise in irrelevancy. She was only twenty-five years old, but what she had gone through stood in sharp contrast with the state of the movement in America and the concerns of her elders. The minutes from the convention are filled with page after page about whether some of the delegates had been rude and hissed when President William Howard Taft addressed them. It was the first time a president had welcomed the convention in all the years they had been meeting in Washington, and the leaders desperately wanted to wish away the alleged hissing as hushing so as to better hear Taft. The offending passage that elicited the unwanted sounds was when Taft said: "If I could be sure that women as a class, including all the intelligent women . . . would exercise the franchise, I should be in favor of it. At present there is considerable doubt." While never acknowledging there had been hissing, the NAWSA sent the president a letter of apology, a bowing to authority that underscored the differences between Paul and the complacency she found when she returned home.

For years there had been a growing chorus of whispers that Anna Shaw was out of touch. Women working in New

York's garment industry had staged a massive walkout in the fall of 1909 that resulted in more than seven hundred arrests, an opportunity for the wealthy, white suffragists to forge a bond with their less-well-off sisters, but Shaw was oblivious and did nothing. Strikes in Chicago and other cities attracted working-class women to the suffrage movement, but Shaw had no instinct for expanding on these inroads. Meanwhile, women in the state of Washington won a referendum in 1910 granting them suffrage, the first state victory in fourteen years, but it was accomplished with almost no help from the NAWSA. Harriot Stanton Blatch, one of Stanton's daughters, found the movement's conservatism so suffocating that she went off on her own to found the New York–based Equality League of Self-Supporting Women. It was dedicated to ordinary women—factory workers and seamstresses—who had for so long been bypassed by the suffrage movement. Within a decade, the league had twenty thousand members.

Women of all ages and classes were becoming receptive to the message of suffrage because modernization and the machine age were making women feel less important as homemakers. They used to run a house in a complex environment. But families were getting smaller and responsibilities less onerous, so women began to search for meaning outside the home. The kitchens of the era look old-fashioned, but they were not fundamentally different from today, whereas an 1860s kitchen might as well have been a prison. If women didn't do the chores, the family couldn't operate. One way women coped with the limits imposed on them by society was their huge consumption of an over-the-counter remedy called laudanum, which was a mix of sherry and aspirin laced with opium. Fragile housewives allegedly needed it to build "strong blood."

The year 1910 turned out to be a watershed one, with the win in Washington paving the way for California in 1911, and Oregon, Arizona, and Kansas in 1912, all voting to give women the ballot. Harriot Blatch changed the name of her organization to the Women's Political Union, and staged the country's first major suffrage parade, on the streets of New York. The press coverage was brutal: marching was considered unladylike behavior, and even many suffragists braced for what they feared would be a backlash. Undaunted, Blatch operated from the dingy basement headquarters of the union, and watched each year as her parade grew in numbers and status. By 1913 almost all the organizations in the city clamored to take part, and an admiring media dubbed the event a "pageant." Ten thousand marchers took part in the parade on Fifth Avenue, while hundreds of thousands of spectators lining the route cheered them on. One in twenty of the marchers was a man. In New York and California, men formed male suffrage leagues, which soon had chapters in twenty-five states.

Presidents then weren't sworn in until March, and when Woodrow Wilson arrived in Washington on the afternoon before his inauguration, he was surprised to see the streets practically empty. "Where are all the people?" he asked. "Oh, everybody's over on the avenue looking at the suffragettes," he was told. Wilson, a prim academic and stubborn moralist, would become the principle antagonist in the final chapter of the long battle for suffrage.

This was Alice Paul's moment. It was March 3, 1913, the eve of the inauguration, and she watched with pride as her handiwork unfolded. Eight thousand women took part in a procession that started at the Capitol, marched up Pennsylvania Avenue past the White House, and ended in a mass rally at the Hall of the Daughters of the American Revolution. Leading the phalanx was a dashingly beautiful young woman on a white horse, Inez Milholland Boissevain, who carried a banner of purple, white, and gold—purple for the royal glory of women, white for purity at home and in politics, gold for the crown of the victor. Paul was a genius at public relations, and she pushed Boissevain to the front of the parade, knowing that her exceptional beauty and ethereal presence—in contrast to the severe and stern image of the early generation of suffragists—would capture the imagination of the movement and the country.

Washington had never seen anything on the magnitude of this procession. Women from countries where suffrage had been granted walked first. Behind them came the "pioneers," women who agitated for the vote as youths and were now well past middle age. Then came sections of marchers, one after the other, honoring the work of women in society. There were nurses in uniform, women farmers and factory workers, homemakers and librarians, college women in academic gowns. Four mounted brigades, more than twenty floats, and nine bands added to the spectacular tableaux. Individual state delegations marched, followed by a separate section for male supporters of woman suffrage, and finally, in a shameful bow to southern segregationist sentiments, at the very back of the parade, a contingent of black women.

The *New York Times* called the event "one of the most impressively beautiful spectacles ever staged in this country." But the pageantry was marred by violence. Paul had a parade permit that entitled the marchers to the streets, but the crowds of men who had gathered did not respect the women's rights and surged onto Pennsylvania Avenue, heckling and jeering the women and making it almost impossible for the parade to pass. The police stood by and did nothing as the women were tripped and shoved, spat at, and had lighted cigarette butts tossed at them. Washington still had a patronage police force, and apparently the officers didn't feel the need to respond professionally even when some of the women were seriously assaulted. The newspapers noted that the police seemed to enjoy and even participated in the "indecent epithets" and "barnyard conversation" hurled at the women. The male marchers fared little better. They were ridiculed with shouts of "Henpecko" and "Where are your skirts?"

Among the marchers was the famed Helen Keller, who had overcome deafness and blindness to become a leading voice for women. The *Chicago Tribune* reported that Keller "was so exhausted and unnerved by the experience in attempting to reach a grandstand" that she was unable to speak later at Constitution Hall. According to the *Tribune* account, two ambulances "came and went constantly for six hours, always impeded and at times actually opposed, so that doctor and driver literally had to fight their way to give succor to the injured." A hundred marchers were taken to the hospital emergency room. The situation deteriorated so badly that Secretary of War Henry Stimson, acting on a plea from the local chief of police, called in troops from nearby Fort Meyer to restrain the rowdy crowd.

The violence made the front page of newspapers all over the country. "Mob Hurts 300 Suffragists at Capital Parade!" screamed the headline in the *New York Evening Journal*. The marchers were mostly young women from respectable homes, and the spectacle of these fragile flowers of femininity, even if they were suffragists, being pushed and shoved by drunken men shouting obscenities proved too much for sedate Washington. There was a congressional investigation, and a Senate committee held several days of hearings during which more than 150 witnesses recounted what they had seen. "There would be nothing like this happening if you would stay at home," one senator chided the marchers. Still, the committee issued a blistering report on the failure of the police to protect the women, and the chief of police in the District of Columbia lost his job.

While she would never have condoned the violence, Paul had to have been secretly pleased. She had created the biggest splash around suffrage the country had seen. All anybody could talk about was the protest; the inauguration the next afternoon of a new president was anticlimactic. The burst of publicity came just when the suffrage movement needed an injection of adrenaline. "Capital Mobs Made Converts to Suffrage" declared the *New York Tribune*.

Paul's hyperawareness of public images had an ugly side. Knowing she needed the support of white Southerners, she relegated black women to the back of the parade to keep them from marching alongside white women. Ida B. Wells-Barnett, a journalist and antilynching crusader, was in Washington representing the all-black Alpha Suffrage Club of Chicago, which she had founded. A suffragist of long standing—she counted Susan B. Anthony as a personal friend—she would not settle for second-class status because of race or gender. She waited on the sidewalk until the Illinois delegation came into view, quietly joining them for the march to the Capitol.

Paul was not the first suffragist to make calculated decisions about excluding blacks to placate whites. In 1894, when Anthony turned down a group of African American women who wanted to form their own chapter and join the NAWSA, it was her friend Wells-Barnett who called her on it, though to no avail. Like Anthony, Paul was immovable once she had fastened on something. Opposition to suffrage in southern states was greater than in the North because of the fear that granting women the vote would increase the black vote exponentially and endanger the southern way of life, which depended on segregation of the races. With the votes of southern legislators in Congress and in the state houses essential if suffrage were ever to become a reality, Paul, and Anthony before her, made a pragmatic if unprincipled decision to keep black women at a distance.

Paul was a human dynamo. Slender and frail-looking as a young woman with skin as pale as alabaster, she had extraordinary energy that seemed to emanate from the swirl of dark hair massed on her head. For a long time she deliberately lived in a cold room so she would not be tempted to stay up late and read, a luxury she felt she could not indulge. The mantelpiece in her bedroom bore visible nicks from where she hung her clothes at night rather than taking an extra few seconds to put them in a closet. She was a woman in a hurry.

When she arrived in Washington in December 1912, eager to work for suffrage, she found that the NAWSA headquarters no longer existed and that most of the contacts she had been given were either dead or had moved away. The wife of a congressman, Mrs. William Kent, who chaired the NAWSA committee ostensibly charged with lobbying for suffrage, had a budget of $10 and no staff. Rather than get discouraged by the situation, Paul saw it as an opportunity. She befriended Mrs. Kent, an older woman who welcomed this eager young woman brimming with energy and ideas. The first thing Paul did was rent a basement office at 1420 F Street, between the Capitol and the White House, to serve as headquarters. A few weeks later, on January 2, 1913, in a small ceremony to inaugurate the space, Mrs. Kent introduced Paul as her successor.

Paul's vision for a pageant to rival Wilson's inauguration did not come cheaply. The senior officers of NAWSA told her to go ahead with her plans, but they would not provide any money. She was the upstart daughter arrived back from England with all these crazy ideas. She was a twentysomething kid who wanted to center suffrage activities in Washington while they were working methodically state by state. Mrs. Kent and the other very-upper-class ladies drawn to the suffrage movement were unaccustomed to scrounging for money, and they did their best selling trinkets at the F Street headquarters. "We have all turned into shopkeepers," one volunteer confided in a letter written during that period. Paul had no compunctions about raising money. She would pursue wealthy women with suffrage sympathies until they wrote a check. And she was creative. Bleachers had been set up along Pennsylvania Avenue for the inaugural parade, and Paul came up with the idea of selling tickets for the suffrage march. This was the pre–civil service era, so there was no government agency involved or oversight of the seating. It was first come, first served for all but the area directly by the White House, which was reserved for the president's family and friends. The incoming administration looked the other way as hustlers parceled out the seats. Paul reportedly made a deal to get half the money collected to help pay for the suffrage march. The total cost of the event, from the twenty-page official program to the elaborate floats and costumes, was $14,906.08, a queen's ransom in 1913, when the average annual wage was just $621.

Paul was often in the company of Lucy Burns, her constant companion and co-conspirator. The two women were opposites in appearance and temperament, just as Anthony and Stanton had been, as though another odd couple had been joined for the final push to suffrage. Whereas Paul appeared fragile, Burns was tall and curvaceous, the picture of vigorous health. She was warm and outgoing, full of Irish charm and with the blue eyes and red hair of her ancestry. Unlike Paul, who was uncompromising and hard to get along with, Burns was more pliable and willing to negotiate. Paul was the militant; Burns, the diplomat. The closeness of their relationship in retrospect raises the possibility that they were more than just friends. Yet nobody then would have suspected lesbianism, because it was so unthinkable. Women could spend time with each other and even share a bed without anybody imagining they had a sexual relationship.

Abolitionists were the first to picket the White House during the Civil War, but Paul's parade was the first time anybody had dared disrupt a presidential inauguration. NAWSA leaders Catt and Shaw didn't know whether to laugh or cry at the exploits of these two young women who had become their assistants. Worried always about whom they might offend, the older women tried to rein in the upstarts, who cared nothing about niceties. They had studied under Mrs. Pankhurst, and upsetting the decorum of Washington was exactly what they wanted to accomplish.

Paul organized a series of visits to the White House beginning on March 17, just days after the inauguration. Presidents were much more accessible then, and Paul wanted to press upon Wilson the importance of suffrage and the imperative that Congress act on the Susan B. Anthony amendment. Wilson received the women, but he played dumb about suffrage, saying he didn't know enough about it and didn't have a position of his own. Besides, Congress was too busy with currency and tariff questions to consider suffrage.

Paul concluded that Wilson would have to be educated, if not embarrassed, into seeing the light. The inside game was half the battle; there had to be pressure from the outside. Relying on the techniques she had learned in Britain, Paul arranged a mass demonstration on April 7, the opening day of a special session of Congress, with suffrage delegates from each of the country's congressional districts carrying petitions demanding passage of the amendment. They marched behind their state banners to the steps of Congress, where they were greeted by sympathetic lawmakers, who then introduced the amendment in both the Senate and the House exactly as it was written and first introduced in 1878. More petitions arrived over the summer in an automobile procession festooned with state flags that culminated at the Capitol and that forced a debate over suffrage in the Senate chamber, the first since 1887.

Emboldened by these events, Paul stepped up the pressure. A new Congress was scheduled to open on December 1; the tariff and currency questions had been resolved; now was the time to approach Wilson anew. But when the White House learned that a delegation of women from New Jersey, Wilson's home state, wanted an appointment, Wilson was suddenly elusive. Paul didn't like the runaround, so she informed White House functionaries that she and the others were on their way. Marching in double file, seventy-three women rounded Pennsylvania Avenue and headed toward the White House. Miraculously, the uniformed guards saluted and made way for the women. Such was the power of protest—and publicity. This time Wilson was a bit frosty at being made to endure the impromptu visit. He still wasn't ready to support suffrage, but he agreed to back the creation of the Committee on Suffrage in the House of Representatives—a small step to be sure, but a step.

The forty-fifth annual convention of the National American Woman Suffrage Association opened in Washington's Columbia Theatre in December 1913, and Lucy Burns unveiled the new strategy that she and Paul had devised. They would hold the party in power responsible. The Democrats controlled the White House and both houses of Congress; the Republicans couldn't deliver suffrage even if they wanted to. It was an ultimatum to the Democrats: pass our bill, or we will defeat you for reelection. "Inaction establishes just as clear a record as does a policy of open hostility," Burns declared. "We have in our hands today not only the weapon of a just case; we have the support of ten enfranchised States—States comprising one-fifth of the United States, one-seventh of the House of Representatives and one-sixth of the electoral vote. More than three million, six hundred thousand women have a vote in presidential elections. It is unthinkable that a national government which represents women . . . should ignore the issue of their right to political freedom."

After telling them he would support the Committee on Suffrage, Wilson neglected to mention it in his message to Congress, rendering his commitment all but worthless. A delegation of fifty-five NAWSA women representing every state quickly assembled to meet with Wilson to register their protest. He claimed illness, forcing the women to wait in Washington through the weekend until he was well enough to receive them. The *Washington Post* reported on December 9 that Wilson informed the delegation he had "set myself a strict rule" that he could not as the leader of the party impose his private views on Congress, and therefore would not urge suffrage legislation on Congress. Wilson's tortured logic gave a green light to the Paul and Burns strategy of holding the Democrats responsible. Enough pressure would eventually be brought that the Democrats—and Wilson himself—would find it expedient to support suffrage rather than continue resisting it.

Early in 1914, the tension between Paul and Catt over the direction of NAWSA came to a head, and Paul broke away from the mother organization. She had been functioning independently anyway as head of the congressional lobbying committee, raising her own money and staging her own protests. When the NAWSA sought to collect a 5 percent tax on her funds as a condition of membership, Paul saw it as an attempt to cripple her activities and, together with a number of radicals and malcontents at the NAWSA, formed the Congressional Union (CU). The CU was extremely active and attracted newcomers to the movement, something the NAWSA had been unable to do for years. The CU organized what today would be called "teach-ins" to educate women about suffrage, and sponsored parades, cross-country "pilgrim hikes," and automobile processions to keep the issue in the public eye. Wilson's position was that the women needed to win suffrage from the state legislatures—not from him, and not from Congress. Wilson was under great stress. His wife, Ellen, his partner and intellectual collaborator for almost thirty years, was ill and increasingly unable to participate in his presidency. She died of kidney disease at age fifty-four on August 2, 1914, amid reports filtering back to the White House of gun battles erupting in Europe. Twelve days later, World War I was officially under way. The freakish double assassination of the archduke of Austria and his wife by a Serbian terrorist triggered the clash of empires that bloodied Europe for four years. Wilson would keep America out of the war until 1917, after he had been safely reelected, but the conflict would consume much of his presidency.

The war diverted attention from suffrage, prompting NAWSA leaders to maneuver ever more carefully around the country's political leaders for fear of appearing unpatriotic. Paul had no such concerns. Her Congressional Union organized and campaigned against all Democratic candidates in the November congressional elections of 1914 for the single reason that the party had not passed the suffrage amendment. CU members went west to the nine states where women had won the vote. They made a huge splash traveling around in hired railroad cars decorated in suffrage colors, and they put a new face on the suffrage movement. These were not the stern aunts of yesteryear; these were attractive young women who dazzled the media with their whistle-stop speeches. When the votes were counted, the CU had defeated twenty Democrats who supported suffrage, a questionable victory in the view of NAWSA leaders, who were heartsick over the outcome. "They have lost our amendment for us; I shall never forgive them," Shaw said. Yet NAWSA had fared little better in advancing the cause. Of the seven campaigns it waged in western and midwestern states in 1914, only two were successful: Nevada and Montana. This boosted the number of suffrage states to eleven, all in the West, where women were scarce and where frontiersmen were willing to do what it took to attract partners.

Paul was undeterred, and when the House of Representatives voted for the first time ever on suffrage the following January, she touted it as a victory even though the amendment lost, 204–174. She was right in the sense that the vote was a historic first, but the lawmakers had their own agenda. This was still the old Congress; the new Congress had not yet been sworn in, and Democrats defeated by the CU wanted to vent their frustration and show Paul who was boss. The amendment would have lost anyway, but the margin was greater than it should have been.

Election Day in November 1915 was a dark day. Suffrage lost in Massachusetts, New York, and Pennsylvania. People had gathered and were mourning the results when Carrie Chapman Catt came out and tried to rally the fallen troops. "We achieved a great victory. More votes were cast for suffrage than ever before," she said. The fight wasn't over; it was just beginning. They immediately passed the hat, collected money, and started again. It would have been human nature to feel defeated, but Catt swallowed hard and went back out and picked up the fight. The suffragists never allowed the opposition to gain the upper hand for long. Still, even the indomitable Catt could not conceal the depth of the defeat in losing three big-state ballot measures on the same day. Somebody had to pay, and that somebody turned out to be Shaw, whose faltering leadership had eroded what was left of her base of support. Shaw resigned, yielding the presidency to Catt, who had been Anthony's original choice for the job. With Wilson's daughter Margaret present as the honorary host at the NAWSA's December convention in Washington, the delegates installed Catt as president and showered Shaw with roses as she stepped down after eleven years of service. Wriggling her head clear of the flowers, Shaw said to thunderous applause, "Men say we are too emotional to vote. But I am very sure that when we compare our emotions in political conventions with the kind they show in theirs, I prefer ours." The *New York Tribune* reported Catt's new watchwords: "Don't Gossip . . . Get Together . . . and Work Hard."

The genteel proceedings struck Paul and her followers as hopelessly out-of-date, and their rift with Catt grew to Grand Canyon size. To make matters worse, the House Judiciary Committee was holding hearings on suffrage at the same time as the NAWSA's convention, dramatizing the split in strategy as the two factions testified on Capitol Hill. The committee chairman, who had been one of the

CU's targets, refused to preside when it was Paul's turn to speak. Dressed like a proper Quaker girl in a long gown of violet silk and a white bib, she didn't look fierce, but she held her ground against the hostile interrogation of a Kansas congressman, Joseph Taggart, angry because his margin of victory had dropped from three thousand votes to three hundred. He couldn't believe her nerve in coming before the committee. "If there was any partisan organization made up of men who had attempted to defeat members of this committee, I do not think we would have given them a hearing," he said. "And if they had been men, they wouldn't have asked for it."

Paul calmly stated her case. The CU was "absolutely nonpartisan." Members included Republicans, Democrats, Socialists, and Progressives united in one thing: putting suffrage first. When the lawmakers pressed her for what she planned to do in the next election, she turned the question back on them, asking what the Democratic Party platform would be in 1916. "I can tell one plank that will not be there, and that is a plank in favor of woman suffrage," a Democrat from North Carolina countered. Paul reminded the lawmakers that a fifth of the vote in the next presidential election would come from suffrage states, clearly implying that she intended no letup in the face of their unyielding opposition. The hearing deteriorated into charges of "cheap politics" and accusations that Paul had "a blacklist" and was doing the bidding of the Republicans.

Paul had already begun choreographing her next big spectacular, the largest-ever petition for suffrage carried across the country by "women automobilists" and presented to Wilson with great fanfare. It would convey 500,000 names and measure 18,333 feet. The convoys began going out during the summer of 1915, and in a country where cars were still a new phenomenon, the sight of these automobile processions winding their way through big cities and small towns, flying the suffrage colors of purple, white, and gold, attracted big crowds and lots of favorable press coverage. The hundred-car procession arrived in Washington to the sound of the "Marseillaise," the French national anthem, and then of "Dixie," stirring music designed to ally the women with anybody within earshot. From the Capitol, the marchers proceeded to the White House with the historic petition unrolled to its full length and borne by twenty women. Wilson received the women in the East Room, and while he had no intention yet of relenting to their demand that he actively press for suffrage, he seemed to be softening. "I am not a man set stiffly beyond the possibility of learning," he said. But with World War I roiling Europe and with America's role in the bloody conflict uncertain, the suffrage debate seemed to Wilson a side matter. His personal life was again in turmoil. He had fallen in love and wanted to remarry, but it had been only nine months since his wife's death. His political aides wanted him to hold off until a more decent interval. Knowing he would resist, they strengthened their case by arguing that his exchange of letters with a woman friend several years earlier hinted at an extramarital affair and that the correspondence would surely leak in the wake of a premature wedding announcement. Wilson agreed to put off the marriage, but he was visibly despondent. In the spring of 1915, when a German U-boat torpedoed the American cruise ship *Lusitania,* pressure mounted on the U.S. government to enter the war, and Wilson turned to his newfound friend for advice. It was the beginning of an extraordinary political partnership between Wilson and Edith Bolling Galt, the forty-three-year-old widow who would soon become his second wife. Wilson rebuffed his aides' pleas to remain single until after his reelection, and on December 18, 1915, he married Edith in a small ceremony at the White House. The couple was inseparable, often beginning the day with a round of golf and working together on war-related matters. Edith became an expert in translating top-secret war codes and often would stay with her husband in the Oval Office, becoming knowledgeable enough about the job to fill in for Wilson when he later became incapacitated.

Meanwhile, the suffrage amendment remained bottled up in the House Judiciary Committee. It was an election year, the committee chairman told Paul. The two major parties were holding their conventions in June, and a grueling campaign lay ahead. Suffrage would have to wait. Paul figured she had wasted a third of the year trying to get these buffoons to perform. It was time to try something different.

She called a meeting for April 8 and 9 at the brownstone they called the "Little White House" and that now served as the CU's headquarters. Paul had wasted no time moving up from the basement quarters she initially rented, and the new space had a proud history. Just across Lafayette Park from the White House, its prime location made it a favorite meeting place for presidents and power brokers of both parties. Signaling a new day, Paul draped the windows with purple, gold, and white, so the suffrage colors could be seen from the White House.

Her idea that April day was to launch an independent political party to advance the goal of suffrage. She wanted to "terrify" the men in Congress with a new party that could rival the clout of Teddy Roosevelt's Bull Moose or Progressive Party, created four years earlier, which had decided the election of 1912 in Wilson's favor. She had given up on effecting change through the existing suffrage groups. After so many decades, lawmakers had grown immune to the perennial pleas for justice and fairness. "Suffrage organizations, unfortunately, have come to stand for feebleness of action and supineness of spirit," Paul said. She called a Woman's Party convention for the summer in Chicago, where both the Republicans and the Progressives were scheduled to meet. Chicago was a media center, and there would be ample publicity.

State groups for the national Woman's Party sprang up almost overnight, and dispatched envoys to the western states to rally women who had the vote to use it for women, and not dilute their power with Republican or Democratic votes. Five thousand people showed up at Washington's Union Station to wish the envoys well. The "Marseillaise" once again rang out, along with "Onward Christian Soldiers" as the charter train began its trip across the country. Labor organizer Eugene Debs was among the crowd when the train stopped in Tucson. In San Francisco, women meeting in the Civic Center stood up as one when asked if they would put suffrage above party affiliation, ringing out, "I will." Harriot Stanton Blatch, following in her mother's footsteps, appealed to a crowd in Seattle, "Ladies, we are here after your votes." When a man's voice rang out, "You'll get them," Blatch shot back, "Men, we need yours, too." The audience applauded.

When the Woman's Party convention opened in Chicago at the Blackstone Theater on July 5, 1916, more than fifteen hundred delegates had registered. Newspaper cartoonists pictured Paul's new party as a frightened deer standing among the elephant, donkey, and bull moose in the competition for electoral primacy. The potential for mischief delighted reporters who were in the city to cover the Republican and Progressive conventions. There were so many requests for tickets to attend a "Suffrage First" luncheon that people settled for standing room only. Among the speakers was Helen Keller, whose inspirational ascent from blindness and deafness was familiar to all, and Inez Milholland Boissevain, the fetching young woman who rode the white horse in the 1913 suffrage parade and whose life would soon be cut short.

The leaders of the NAWSA worried that Paul's exploits would be counterproductive and cost them the friends in high places they had worked so long to cultivate. In a last attempt to bridge the divide, the two factions met at Washington's Willard Hotel but failed to reach any accommodation. Paul wouldn't back down from her strategy of holding the party in power responsible, while Catt insisted that suffrage could be won more decorously in a state-by-state strategy combined with gentle pressure on the powers that be. She said she had devised a "winning plan," but she refused to divulge any of its specifics. The younger women aligned with Paul looked on Catt as an out-of-date dinosaur. They were children when she won her historic victories in western elections, and they had no confidence in her or her secret plan.

Neither Paul nor Catt could have known it then, but they needed each other. Paul injected the energy and chutzpah the movement needed to force Congress and President Wilson to act. Catt quietly worked the levers of power to capture the moment. Without her surefooted diplomacy and relentless organization, the required two-thirds of state legislatures would not have ratified suffrage.

The country was uneasy about the prospect of war, and Wilson was seeking reelection with the assumption (mistaken, it turned out) that he would keep America out of the conflagration that was consuming Europe. Wilson had a formidable foe in former U.S. Supreme Court Justice Charles Evans Hughes, who had left the High Court to campaign for the presidency. Prodded by the politics of a tough reelection contest, Wilson pledged in a letter to Catt in June 1916 that the Democratic Party would include a suffrage endorsement in its platform. This was a huge step for Wilson because it committed him to the activist role he had so long avoided under the guise of principle. But contrary to what Catt expected, Wilson hadn't moved that much. When the Democrats held their convention that summer in St. Louis, the platform as offered by Wilson still left suffrage up to the states, echoing the Republican position. Disappointed in both major parties, Catt and Paul kept up the pressure. Hughes was inundated by mail from angry women, and found his image as a fair and just jurist under withering attack in newspaper editorials. Hughes caved first, sending a telegram on August 1 to Utah senator George Sutherland, a longtime backer of suffrage, to declare his support for a federal amendment. It was the first time a presidential candidate from either of the two major parties endorsed the amendment.

The NAWSA typically met late in the year, in November or December, but Catt called an emergency convention for early September in Atlantic City. She wanted maximum exposure before the elections for her "winning plan," a strategy that focused on state suffrage referendums. Catt's idea was deceptively simple. They would target states where they had a good chance of winning. Before that, state campaigns had been haphazard. Catt brought a strategic eye to the battle. "The woman's hour has struck," she told the delegates. Both presidential candidates were invited to speak in Atlantic City, but only Wilson accepted, and he insisted on speaking last. He lectured like the professor he once was, reminding the delegates that women first became prominent in politics in America because of the slavery question, and that the country was now facing another great social question with suffrage. "It is going to prevail," he declared, describing himself as getting "a little impatient sometimes about the discussion of the channels and methods by which it is going to prevail."

By October, Wilson and seven of his ten cabinet members had come out for suffrage, but he was vague when asked whether it would be realized in his second term. The Woman's Party continued to picket Wilson throughout the campaign. The NAWSA was more cautious. Suffrage was an important issue, but voters were jittery over the possibility of U.S. involvement in the European war, which was now well under way, having begun in 1914. Many Woman's Party members were determined pacifists, and Catt and company did not want to align the NAWSA with any issue other than suffrage.

Faithful to the techniques she had learned in Britain, Alice Paul did not veer from the course she had set of holding the party in power responsible for the stalemate on suffrage. The Woman's Party dispatched "girl organizers" to the twelve western states where women were allowed to vote. Their message: anybody but the Democrats. They didn't care if women voted for Republicans, Socialists, or Prohibitionists, only that they denied their vote to the Democrats. If a large enough protest vote could be mobilized, no party in power would ever again dismiss suffrage. A stream of speakers fanned out to the western states. They were the best and the brightest of the suffrage movement, and among them was the brilliant and beautiful Inez Milholland Boissevain. She had been named a "special flying envoy," which meant she planned to visit all twelve western suffrage states.

Wilson campaigned on the slogan "He kept us out of war." The Woman's Party countered with "He kept us out of suffrage."

6

Martyr for the Cause

By October, Inez Milholland Boissevain had spoken in Wyoming, Idaho, Oregon, Washington, Montana, Utah, Nevada, and California. Her trip had not been easy: a train at two in the morning to arrive at eight; then a train at midnight to arrive at five in the morning. "She would come away from audiences and droop as a flower," Maud Younger, a women's labor organizer who traveled with her, recalled. "She would ride in the trains gazing from the windows, listless, almost lifeless, until one spoke; then again the sweet smile, the sudden interest, the quick sympathy. The courage of her was marvelous." At an October rally in Los Angeles, Boissevain was quoting one of Wilson's many paeans to democracy: "The tide is rising to meet the moon; you will not have long to wait."

"Mr. President, how much longer must women wait for liberty?" she cried out. With the word "liberty" still on her lips, she collapsed in a faint to the floor. There was speculation that she had leukemia, or some terrible fever, or that she had simply given out because of the strain. Whatever

113

the reason, she was dead ten weeks later, a martyr for the cause. She was thirty years old.

On the defensive over Boissevain's untimely passing, Alice Paul offered this statement: "When the men speakers go out on such long campaign trips, they have private cars and physical directors to care for them. Our girls traveled on small allowances, often taking upper berths and going without many of the comforts of travel. They had to travel long distances at night to lose no time during the day when they could be making speeches." Paul's remarks prompted this chiding response from the *Louisville (Ky.) Times:* "There are many activities and exigencies in life for which women are better fitted than are men. It is doubtful that political campaigning is one of them. Women have not been at this business long enough to obtain the psychic support which the clamor of the hustings gives the men. . . . The *Times* deplores any form of activity in politics for the women of either party which is to result in disablement and death."

For all her delicate beauty, Boissevain was a seasoned radical and determined suffragist. As a student at Vassar, she held a suffrage meeting in a graveyard at night when the school refused her permission to use the college chapel for the meeting. She was captain of her class hockey team, a member of the track team, and the holder of an 8-pound shotput record with 31 feet, ⁷⁄₈ inch. On her first college vacation, she traveled to London where, like Paul, she became enamored of the Pankhursts and once was arrested. During the 1908 presidential campaign she had her first taste of fame when the newspapers wrote her up as "the girl who broke up the Taft parade." While Republican contender William Howard Taft and his supporters marched by, Inez Milholland, safely ensconced in a high window, shouted "Votes for Women!" through a megaphone. This was daring behavior for the times, and scores of marchers fell out of the parade to hear more from the fetching young woman in the window.

After graduating from Vassar, Milholland applied to Harvard Law School but was denied admission because she was a woman. The rejection only spurred her activism, and she joined the shirtwaistmakers' strike in New York, where she was arrested and held for several weeks before the charge against her of leading an unlawful assembly was dropped. She was featured regularly in news accounts as "the most beautiful suffragette," an appellation that never turned her head, or lessened her interest in her studies. She earned a law degree from New York University in 1912, and started her career as a criminal defense attorney in New York. In July 1913 she married Eugene Boissevain, a wealthy European from Holland, whom she had met through Guglielmo Marconi, the inventor of the wireless telegraph. Not that Milholland lacked for anything—her family had money—but the merger with Boissevain further ensured that she could continue her suffrage activities uninterrupted by financial concerns.

She traveled at will, and accumulated a worldwide reputation as a suffragist and pacifist. In 1915 her alma mater, Vassar, refused to allow her to speak in favor of suffrage during the college's fiftieth anniversary ceremonies. Later that same year, with war raging in Europe, she was forced to leave Italy because of her passionate writings in favor of pacifism.

This was no fragile flower who had wilted when the train travel took its toll. When Paul asked the equally eloquent and well-traveled Maud Younger to deliver the memorial address for Boissevain, Younger, never at a loss for words, panicked at the enormity of the task. "I can't," she said. "I don't know how to do it." Paul's breezy response did not lessen Younger's fear, but it also left no room to disappoint: "Oh, just write something like Lincoln's Gettysburg Address," she said with a characteristic wave of her hand.

Inez Milholland Boissevain was buried on a quiet hillside in upstate New York, where she was born, and arrangements were made for a memorial service in Washington. Paul decided that the most fitting place to commemorate this fallen suffragist was Statuary Hall in the U.S. Capitol, a marble-columned chamber lined with statues of America's heroes and off-limits for memorial services except for those already honored in the hall. (No woman would be included until 1997, when a statue of three suffragists was hauled up from the Capitol basement amid much controversy and given a rightful place in the hall.) Paul predictably did not take no for an answer and proceeded with plans for the service. So great were her powers of persuasion that as the appointed hour approached, one by one, the obstacles posed by the authorities melted away, and the Capitol police could be seen helping to place the trademark purple, white, and gold suffrage pennants around the chamber.

With her eye for pageantry, Paul arranged a glorious send-off for Boissevain. The memorial service was held on Christmas Day 1916, and the vibrant greens of the season served as the backdrop to the suffrage colors. As the guests took their seats, an organ played "Ave Maria," and a boys choir paraded slowly into the hall. They were followed by a suffragist carrying a duplicate of the banner Inez Milholland had held aloft in the first suffrage parade in New York, in 1912, and then a procession of young women dressed first all in purple, then white, then gold, each division bearing a golden suffrage banner. The sweet voices of the young boys filled the chamber, followed by speeches of tribute. Maud Younger summoned up a poetic remembrance of her compatriot, "a falling star in the western heavens," and urged that Boissevain's sacrifice inspire the cause of suffrage: "that dying she shall bring to pass that which living she could not achieve, full freedom for women, full democracy for the nation. . . ." The organ sounded the triumphal chords of the "Marseillaise," and the battle was once again engaged.

Though Wilson was reelected in 1916 with an antiwar theme, he had come to believe that U.S. participation in World War I was inescapable. He was uncomfortable with the antiwar rhetoric generated at the Democratic convention, but not so uncomfortable that he didn't exploit it at the same time he was readying for war. The buzzword of the time was "preparedness." America needed to be ready. Wilson prepared the country to enter the war with lofty speeches about preserving freedom and democracy. Against this rhetoric, his refusal to champion the right of half the U.S. population to vote gave the suffragists the opening they needed to undertake round-the-clock vigils at the White House and denounce "Kaiser Wilson" as a hypocrite.

Illinois was the only state that counted the votes of women separately, and over seventy thousand more women voted against Wilson than for him, the first recorded evidence of the gender gap that would become a feature of modern American politics. Suffrage leaders noted another development: there were 864 dance halls connected with saloons in the city of Chicago alone. A month after woman suffrage passed in Illinois, many had closed. "Don't make much of the saloons," a NAWSA leader counseled. Getting aligned with the prohibition movement would only alienate male voters.

Wilson handily won reelection, carrying all but one of the other eleven states where women could vote. Paul dismissed criticism that her Woman's Party campaign had been a failure. Her goal was to put western Democrats on the defensive over suffrage, which she believed she had accomplished. Jeanette Rankin, an unabashed feminist and former staff member of the NAWSA, was elected to the House of Representatives from Montana largely on the strength of a prosuffrage and antiwar vote among women. The first woman to win federal elective office, Rankin was one of fifty members of Congress to vote against U.S. entry into World War I, which resulted in her defeat after a single term. Rankin was reelected years later, and in a quirk of history was in Congress to cast the only vote in the House against U.S. involvement in World War II. "You can no more win a war than you can win an earthquake," she said. Though Rankin is legitimately held up as a hero for women, her staunch pacifism fed the stereotype that women shrink from war even when it's necessary and therefore can't be entrusted with matters of national security.

Rankin had been a NAWSA lobbyist, and when she was first in Congress, lived in Suffrage House, a stone mansion on Rhode Island Avenue about six blocks from the White House and that served as NAWSA headquarters. Her vote in 1917 against the war epitomized the growing tension between suffrage and patriotism. Catt also was a dedicated pacifist, but once Wilson declared war, she put aside all her peace activities and threw herself into war work. Suffragists at every level felt enormous pressure to show the flag for the war effort. They did home canning, raised money to buy ambulances, set up canteens in rail stations for trains carrying troops, and operated a port kitchen in Hoboken, New Jersey, that over a period of seven months served more than 1 million returning soldiers and sailors. An antisuffragist society in Massachusetts, wanting to keep pace with the visible contributions of suffragists, sent out a letter in March 1918 to all its chapters asking for "the names of women doing Red Cross, Surgical Dressing or any other kind of war work." The letter also requested "comparative data to suffragists if available."

What to do with all the women who wanted to help was an issue for which the administration was ill prepared. Government's response when it doesn't know what else to do is to create a committee. In this case, it was the Woman's Committee of the Council of National Defense. Anna Howard Shaw was the chairperson, and Catt was one of ten on the committee. The committee's tasks were vague, and its members mostly prepared reports that went unread. Irrelevant as the work was, Catt was seen as a patriot, while Paul stayed on the war's sidelines. Catt and Paul were increasingly at odds. Catt didn't buy into the British-based theory of defeating pro-suffrage Democrats because the party didn't get behind the amendment. She thought the picketing hardened the opposition on Capitol Hill and that gentle persuasion was a more useful tool in winning converts than Paul's radical displays. Though on the rare occasions when the two women saw each other, they were civil, both understood that they were engaged in a historic slugfest. Catt had the establishment on her side. The New York State Woman Suffrage Party came out publicly against the "small group of insurgents who seceded from the main body of suffragists over two years ago. Both New York and NAWSA have repeatedly asked them to give up their picketing of the White House and have officially expressed their condemnation of these tactics as tending to harass the president in this time of great stress."

When Wilson read his State of the Union address before a joint session of Congress, the sudden unveiling of a yellow suffrage banner in the gallery interrupted the somber occasion. "Mr. President, what will you do for woman suffrage?" The banner was aloft for no more than a few seconds before it was torn from the hands of the six suffrage workers who had defied the rules by displaying it.

That evening, as Wilson dined with members of the Gridiron Club, a society of journalists, the same golden banner reappeared, "clutched in the grip of a person as elaborately garbed as any Paris fashion model," according to a news account. The club's president leaped to his feet and dashed to disarm the beauteous protester while a policeman struggled to remove her from the ballroom. The three hundred diners gasped before arriving at the realization this was one of the jokes the club was known for springing on its political guests. Both the alleged suffragist and the uniformed policeman were journalists playing roles. But how the banner arrived at the dinner remained a subject of mystery, since it had been confiscated earlier in the day by the sergeant at arms of the House and supposedly entrusted to his safekeeping.

Wilson's reaction was most intriguing. When he first saw the banner unfurl in the House gallery, reporters thought they detected a very faint smile as he went on with his speech. There was no break in his composure. That evening, as he watched the Gridiron parody, Wilson laughed with gusto, revealing that for all his rigid composure, he had a sense of humor about the pressure campaign aimed at him.

That December evening, as 1916 drew to a close, may have been the last time Wilson found anything to laugh about. A January reception in the White House for three hundred women who were carrying resolutions from around the country memorializing Inez Milholland

Boissevain ended in a tense standoff as the women pressed the president "to end this wasteful struggle of women" and Wilson stubbornly held his ground. "It is impossible for me, until the orders of my party are changed, to do anything other than what I am doing as a party leader," he said. The women felt that they had once again gotten the brush-off and responded to the president's words with silence. Wilson appeared flustered. He waited for a moment; then he turned and left.

The women walked out into the frigid January air and made their way across Lafayette Park to the Woman's Party headquarters, where they held what amounted to a revival meeting. Despair turned to a spirited call for a renewed militancy focused almost entirely on the one man who had just rebuffed their pleas. Harriot Stanton Blatch put it to the crowd of women who had gathered: "Never before did the Democratic Party lie more in the hands of one man than it lies today in the hands of President Wilson. He controls his party, and I don't think he is too modest to know it. He can mold it as he wishes and yet he is not willing to lay a finger's weight on his party today for half the people of the United States," she concluded. "Women, it rests with us. . . . Let us stand beside the gateway where he must pass in and out, so that he can never fail to realize that there is a tremendous earnestness and insistence back of this measure." Blatch urged each woman to become a "silent sentinel" in the president's midst, a call to action that within minutes resulted in raising $3,000 to fund the expanded vigils.

The first picket line at the White House appeared on January 10, 1917; the last, more than a year and a half

later. With rare exceptions, they were the
except Sunday, taking their place at the White H
with military precision and maintaining a statuelike
all kinds of weather and despite harassments fr
passersby. Competing with war news from Europe and the
impending entry of America's armed forces in the conflict
was a challenge. Paul kept up media interest in these
"silent sentinels" by highlighting certain states, or bringing
in college students, and even designating one Sunday
"Labor Day" so women who worked in factories or offices
could participate on their only day off.

Wilson initially tolerated and was even a bit amused at
the women permanently stationed outside the White
House gates. On cold days he told the guards to invite
them in for coffee, which they refused. When his car drove
through the picket line, he would tip his hat to the
women as though thanking them for moving peaceably
aside. Sometimes he even smiled. But with America about
to enter the war and the women throwing his own words
back at him and ridiculing his commitment to democracy,
his patience was coming to an end.

When Inez Milholland Boissevain died, Paul immediately wrote to Boissevain's younger sister, Vida, imploring
her to "join the crusade." Vida Milholland answered the
call, and on March 4, 1917—Inauguration Day—she led a
march of nearly a thousand picketers around the White
House. They circled the perimeter of the grounds four
times for a distance of four miles, with Vida carrying a
golden banner with her sister's last known words: "Mr.
President, how long must women wait for liberty?" Behind

...ft what the women called ... said simply, "We demand ...ation of the United States ...he floodgates opened as a ... the various states followed ...ag amid a drenching rain as ...rchers.

...then as it is today, so the women were surprised ... l all the White House gates locked, and their access to the building denied. The guards would only promise to present the calling cards of the women at the end of the day, their customary procedure when uninvited guests showed up. The weather had deteriorated to sleet and near-gale-force winds, but the women persisted, their hands blue with the cold. Some fainted or fell with exhaustion and had to be carried off to waiting automobiles. When President and Mrs. Wilson emerged in the late afternoon in their limousine, they fixed their eyes straight ahead so they could avoid seeing the long line of marchers to the left and right. Photos that ran the following day in the nation's leading newspapers showed the picketers, umbrellas aloft, surrounding the White House and trying in vain to gain entry. It was the first action undertaken by the newly named "National Woman's Party," Paul's way of serving notice that the two organizations she had created—the Congressional Union and the Woman's Party—were now one. The campaign for suffrage had moved from the West to Washington.

As a special war session of Congress opened on April 2, 1917, picketers stationed themselves at the entrance of the

House and Senate as well as maintaining their presence at the White House. By this time, nineteen states had granted women the right to vote. Suffrage was a sidebar to the national debate about war versus peace. Pacifists wearing white badges swarmed Congress in a last desperate effort to hold off war. On April 7, Congress declared the nation at war with Germany. Wilson echoed the sentiment expressed on Capitol Hill with these memorable words: "We shall fight for the things which we have always held nearest our hearts—for democracy—for the right of those who submit to authority to have a voice in their own governments."

Many suffragists volunteered to help in the war effort, and in New York State, where a referendum campaign was under way, street meetings and parades were canceled in deference to the war. A million men were sent to the European front, and another million were readied to go. Suffragists plunged into war gardening and feeding the soldiers at military bases. First lady Edith Wilson, wearing a Red Cross uniform, would see off the troops mustering for duty at Washington's Union Station. Food and fuel had to be conserved, and to set an example, Edith brought a flock of twenty sheep to graze on the White House lawn, auctioning off their wool to raise money for the Red Cross. Hollywood celebrities such as Charlie Chaplin and Mary Pickford appeared with the first lady to urge Americans to buy war bonds. The only overt suffrage campaigning in New York was the gathering of signatures. Women went house to house with petitions until they had secured more than a million signatures, a feat that finally silenced those who said that women do not want the vote.

Then came the parade, a huge event on Fifth Avenue filled with marching women in blue and gray uniforms, ready to be deployed overseas, or with white on their heads to symbolize bandages and caring for the wounded men. The newspapers said it was not a suffrage parade; it was "a woman's parade." Mothers with the service stars of their fallen sons were in the front, followed by women who had answered the call of their country by filling in for the absent men. There were women census takers, women police, women chauffeurs, "conductorettes and farmerettes," according to news reports. It was an impressive display of the value of women in wartime, and when the votes were counted, suffrage passed in New York with a decisive majority of 140,000 votes. Catt had been able to under-write the campaign with generous checks for $10,000 and $15,000, the result of an unexpected bequest from Mrs. Frank Leslie, a wealthy publisher and lifetime suffragist who upon her death left almost $1 million to Catt and NAWSA. Leslie had danced at Abraham Lincoln's first Inaugural Ball and led a colorful life during which she inherited *Leslie's Illustrated Weekly* from her third husband and built it into an empire with thirteen publications that reached into almost every American home. She had written a fan letter to Susan B. Anthony in 1888 and given modest contributions to NAWSA, but nobody anticipated such a sizable contribution. Her late husband's relatives contested the will, but in the end Catt was awarded the money.

Catt and the NAWSA leaders begged Paul to recall the White House pickets and suspend her suffrage activities for the war's duration. She turned aside the pleas, reminding her critics that women had backed off once before in the face of war, and when the Civil War was over, black men could vote and white women were told to wait. She wasn't going to fall into that trap, and announced in an editorial in the *Suffragist* that the National Woman's Party would continue to press for federal action on suffrage. Individual members were free to donate their time to the war effort, but the party would focus exclusively on suffrage. For five months, from January through May, the picketers kept up their vigil unimpeded in front of the White House. They became a tourist attraction, and visitors to the city would ask to hold a banner and pose among the women for a picture.

The politicians assumed that when the weather turned bitter cold, that would drive away the protesters. Instead, the janitor who worked at headquarters across the park would heat bricks, cover them with gunnysack, and trundle them across Pennsylvania Avenue in a wheelbarrow so the women could stand on them and warm their feet. The White House guards befriended the women, treating them like an auxiliary security force patrolling the same beat. Once, when the women were a few minutes late, one of the guards said: "We thought you weren't coming, and we'd have to hold down this place alone."

With the outbreak of war, the White House gates were regularly locked for the first time in the nation's history. But there was such a level of trust between the guards and the women that when Wilson emerged in his limousine for his afternoon ride, the police would shout to the onlookers who had gathered, "Back! Back! All back but the pickets!"

The women who dedicated their time were for the most part women of leisure who, if they weren't picketing, would be doing charity work or attending afternoon teas, a prized feature of Washington social life for the upper classes. Mrs. William Kent, the wife of a congressman and a steadfast friend to Paul, regarded the picketing as a form of public service and made a habit of excusing herself early from Monday teas. "I picket Mondays from two to six," she explained.

The picketing was surprisingly genteel, which was a false precursor of the brutality that lay ahead. This was a time to savor, a time of sweet civility. Various dignitaries after meeting with Wilson would smile their approval at the suffragists. Former president Teddy Roosevelt beamed broadly when he passed through the gate, waving his hat in what the women took to be a gesture of solidarity. When a reunion of Confederate soldiers convened in Washington, many of the aged veterans came by to pay their respects. Their view of the suffragists, never favorable in the past, had changed. These women had fortitude and perseverance, qualities men had to admire.

It was a sunny June day in 1917 when the mood shifted. A car carrying Russian diplomats was expected at the White House, and two silent sentinels stood at the gate awaiting their arrival. They held a lettered banner that read: "To the Russian envoys, we the women of America tell you that America is not a democracy. Twenty million American women are denied the right to vote. President Wilson is the chief opponent of their national enfranchisement. Help us make this nation really free. Tell our government it must liberate its people before it can claim free Russia as an ally." These were crucial talks for Wilson, who was trying to persuade the Russians, newly liberated from czarist oppression, to continue in the war on the side of America for democracy. One of Wilson's envoys had visited Moscow and bragged of his country's "universal, direct, equal, and secret suffrage."

There was media speculation, no doubt fed by Paul, that the suffragists would make a direct appeal to the Russian visitors, and a crowd had gathered in anticipation of a possible clash. As soon as the diplomats passed through the gate, somebody in the crowd tore down the banner. The same thing happened the next day with a replacement banner. The police looked on but did nothing to stop the vandalism. Paul and the women faced renewed criticism that they were embarrassing their president in front of foreign visitors and impeding the war effort. Paul did not flinch. She said the fault was with Wilson and not the women "if the lack of democracy at home weakens the administration in its fight for democracy three thousand miles away."

Wilson was embarrassed, and he wanted a stop put to the picketing. A number of solutions were considered, including having a military zone established around the White House and closing down the National Woman's Party headquarters, but these were extreme steps and they would be hard to justify. Wilson settled instead for a policy of having the women arrested if they continued to picket. Paul was philosophical at first, explaining what had happened with this metaphor. "If a creditor stands before a man's house all day long, demanding payment of his bill,

the man must either remove the creditor or pay the bill."
By ordering the arrests, Wilson sought to remove the
source of his torment. He would eventually honor the bill.

Paul had consulted with lawyers and knew the women
had a legal right to picket. The next day the women carried
a banner to the White House with Wilson's own words:
"We shall fight for the things which we have always held
nearest our hearts—for democracy—for the right of those
who submit to authority to have a voice in their own governments." A crowd had gathered, anticipating that there
would be arrests, but the police did not interfere with the
women. Eventually the crowd dissipated, and when the
avenue in front of the White House was completely
deserted, the police made their move. Lucy Burns and a
fellow suffragist, Katherine Morey of Brookline, Massachusetts, were led away and taken to the police station.
When the women asked what they were being charged
with, the police officials had no answer. Picketing is a guar-
anteed right under the law. Hours passed before the
women were told they had obstructed the traffic on Pennsylvania Avenue. It was such a blatantly phony charge that
the women were released on their own recognizance and
never brought to trial.

The arrests continued the next day with the same result,
and it was clear the administration hoped to suppress the
pickets with a strategy of harassment. Finding women with
the time and the inclination to picket was difficult enough
when everything was peaceful. Once the arrests started, it
became harder to find fresh reinforcements to replenish
the line. More than two dozen women were arrested in

See
125

five days. When simply detaining the pickets failed to deter them, the government upped the ante and decided to bring the last six women arrested to trial. On June 27, six American women were tried in the police court of the District of Columbia and found guilty of obstructing traffic. They were ordered to pay $25 or serve three days in the D.C. jail for what the court said was "unpatriotic, almost treasonable behavior."

The women defended themselves and asked that their banner be entered as evidence. There was chuckling in the courtroom when a policeman was ordered to carry in the tattered purple, white, and gold suffrage banner. "Not a dollar of your fine shall we pay," the women asserted. "To pay a fine would be an admission of guilt. We are innocent." When these first pickets came out of jail, a hundred women were waiting to greet them and toast them at a garden breakfast reception.

The next picket line went out on Independence Day, July 4, 1917, and included Vida Milholland, whose sister was martyred for the cause. They marched across Lafayette Park from headquarters carrying a yellow banner that read, "Governments derive their just power from the consent of the governed." Following the dictum of the court, they kept moving so as not to obstruct traffic, but before they could even reach the White House, the police stopped them. A minor melee broke out as onlookers surged forward to grab the banners and another contingent of strategically placed suffragists suddenly appeared on the other side of Pennsylvania Avenue, a magnet for further disruption. The police eventually restored order using strong-arm tactics, and the women were booked for "unlawful assembly." Again they conducted their own defense, insisting their torn yellow banner be brought into the court, and throughout the trial, it hung suspended from the judge's bench with its suffrage message. Lucy Burns summed up the case for the defense, noting that there is no law against carrying banners through the streets of Washington, and that the arrests appeared to have nothing to do with violating any District laws, but were intended to suppress the suffrage appeal to the president. The verdict: Guilty with a choice of a $25 fine or three days in jail.

The day after the verdict was Bastille Day, and the National Woman's Party announced in a press release that it would carry a banner with the French national motto "Liberty, Equality, Fraternity" to the White House. This was another act of defiance, and the police swept up all the picketers, sixteen women in total, booking them for unlawful assembly. With wave after wave of women coming before his court, Judge Edward O'Hearn Mullowney was losing his patience. This time the sentence would not be so light. The women were sentenced to sixty days in Occoquan Workhouse. The charge was obstructing traffic.

Among the imprisoned protesters was the sister-in-law of former secretary of war Stimson. Details of the workhouse conditions immediately leaked, and Paul disseminated them to the media and to her activist network. The women were locked up in the same quarters with women who had criminal records, and forced to sleep in the same dormitory with black women, revelations that shook the sensibilities of upper-class Washington. News reports pointed out that the women came from fine families and were unaccustomed to such crudities. A New Jersey man who had worked for Wilson's reelection and whose wife was among the imprisoned gained an audience with Wilson that made the front pages. Wilson pronounced himself "shocked" by the conditions as they were described to him. The *New York World* of July 17, 1917, reported that Wilson assured his visitor that he "feels the situation keenly" and would consider treating the suffrage amendment as a war emergency measure.

This was a key concession, since the Democrats who controlled Congress had announced they would deal with nothing that was not directly connected to the war.

The newspapers were filled with detailed descriptions of life at the Occoquan Workhouse, and it wasn't pretty. Breakfast at 7:00 A.M. in the main dining hall, with the Negro prisoners on one side, and whites on the other. Warden William H. Whittaker placed one white prisoner between each of the suffragists so that communication became almost impossible. After breakfast of fried hominy with gravy, some women were sent outdoors to the garden to pick blackberries—backbreaking work—while others were ordered to the sewing room. "But suppose we don't know how to sew," one said. These were upper-class women who had servants to do their needlework. "That is something we will soon teach you," the warden replied with more than a touch of smugness. The suffragists sewed all day, making overalls, underwear, and bedclothes for the prisoners, breaking only for meals of beef and cabbage. The *New York World* reported that the husband of Mrs. Gilson Gardner, a well-known newspaper writer who had backed Wilson, feared his wife could not handle the prison food. He despaired over the gray prison garb worn by previous prisoners and sanitized for the newcomers. "A man would not recognize his wife in them," he said. Yet he did not pay her fine to gain her release, knowing that was not what she would want. Another husband, commenting on the food, said, "What is good for a drunken Negro is not good for a refined woman." When a member of Congress phoned the prison asking if he could send the women a box of California fruit, Warden Whittaker denied the request. No special favors, he said.

Reading the news coverage, Wilson knew he had lost the public relations battle. The National Woman's Party was papering the country with press releases, each one making him look worse. "As long as the government and its representatives prefer to send women to jail on petty and technical charges to giving women justice, we will go to jail," members of the New York chapter announced. "Persecution has always advanced the cause of liberty," they declared to waiting media.

After just three days, Wilson capitulated. "Militants in Jail Pardoned by President," announced the headline in the *New York Evening Sun* of July 19, 1917; "16 Suffrage pickets now free to leave Washington Work House; will continue their work; Announce they will picket White House once a week—Pardon is unconditional." The women had been sentenced to sixty days' imprisonment, so this was quite a reprieve. But it did not, as Wilson hoped, lessen their militant stand. The women accepted the pardons "under protest," vowing to continue "the agitation" regardless of where it led. Mrs. J. A. H. Hopkins, whose husband had worked for Wilson and been a member of the Democratic National Committee, wrote Wilson a personal letter to say that the pardon in no way made up for the ongoing denial of her civil rights. Then she marched over to the White House and resumed her vigil with a banner that said, "We ask not pardon for ourselves but justice for all American women." A crowd gathered, but the police left her undisturbed. As she stood there, Wilson passed through the White House gates, politely saluting as though nothing were amiss.

Wilson bought himself some time with the wider public by pardoning the women. It was wartime, and the women's antics were seen by many as an unnecessary distraction. A cheerleading press did not challenge the administration's ban on showing pictures of dead soldiers, shielding the public from the worst of war and taking its cues from Washington. An editorial in the *Brooklyn Eagle* headlined "An Unwise Suffrage Campaign" said that until the war was won, not an ounce of energy should be expended on anything other than supplying men, munitions, and food. The editorial likened the focus on suffrage to spotting a fly on the door and concentrating on the fly instead of the door. Carrie Chapman Catt wrote an open letter disapproving of the picketing and the tactics of the National Woman's Party. She called it "an error of judgment." Catt busied herself and the NAWSA during this period with state campaigns, which didn't attract nearly the same level of hostility from the politicians or the press as Paul's push for a federal amendment.

In the immediate aftermath of Wilson's pardons, there was a truce of sorts. The police relaxed their surveillance of the suffragists, and the women resumed their daily vigils without fear of arrest. Government workers who passed by the White House on their way home in the afternoon were amused to see the suffragists return. Some congratulated the women at triumphing over the system. But the benign neglect wasn't helping the cause. With the heat off, Wilson did nothing to advance an amendment in Congress. Then an opportunity arose. Elihu Root, Wilson's special envoy to Russia, was due at the White House. Russia had enfranchised its women, and there was rivalry between the two nations. When Root arrived, he was confronted by a manifesto in the form of a banner. It said in part: "This nation is not free. . . . Tell the President that he cannot fight against liberty at home while he tells us to fight for liberty abroad. . . . Tell him to make America free for democracy before he asks the mothers of America to throw their sons to the support of democracy in Europe."

The largest crowd the pickets had ever attracted looked on expectantly as the suffragists maintained their vigil with the banner for a full two hours. The sidewalk by the White House was completely congested, yet the police did not interfere, and the crowd was peaceable. The women didn't know quite what to make of this new laissez-faire attitude.

They got their answer the next day, August 14, the beginning of the most violent period in the history of the pickets and of the suffrage movement. "Kaiser Wilson:

Take the beam out of your own eye" taunted a new suffrage banner. The women wanted to remind Wilson of the contradiction between his prodemocracy rhetoric and his policies. He was willing to go to war to defend the right of the German people to self-government, but he was keeping 20 million American women under his boot. Germany was the enemy. Anti-German sentiment was so strong in the United States during World War I that orchestras refused to play Beethoven, sauerkraut was renamed liberty cabbage, and frankfurters became hot dogs. Invoking the phrase "Kaiser Wilson" was like pouring kerosene on a fire. Rioting broke out almost immediately and drove the women back to their headquarters, where they hung a banner out the second-floor window, further inflaming the passions of the unruly crowd. The police did nothing to quell the disturbance. "Why don't you arrest those men?" one of the suffrage leaders asked a policeman. "Those are not our orders," he replied. The low point came late in the afternoon when someone in the crowd fired a bullet through the second-floor window, which fortunately did not hit anybody.

The women were back picketing the next two days, with more banners amid more mob violence. Sailors in uniform led the melee on one day, and the police egged on the rioters the next day. A sailor knocked Alice Paul to the ground and dragged her across the sidewalk as he yanked off her suffrage sash. Hundreds of suffrage banners were destroyed and shredded, and several women were shoved to the pavement and had their clothes torn. Yet the women showed no indication that they would back down.

They concealed banners inside their sweaters and hats, or folded them up in newspapers and pinned them under their skirts. Lucy Burns organized relays of fresh banners to replace those that had been destroyed. The long struggle for the vote was reaching a climax, and it was a thrilling time. Wilson, watching from the White House, was perplexed and angry. He had lost face when the women were initially arrested and treated like common prisoners, and he had regained some measure of dignity, he thought, by generously pardoning the suffragists. Instead of being grateful, they had exploited their freedom.

After three days of August riots, Wilson decided it was time to once again crack down. On the morning of August 17, the District of Columbia chief of police called Paul to alert her that he had new orders to immediately arrest women carrying banners. "The pickets will go on as usual," Paul told him. That same morning, the silent sentinels stood in front of the White House with these banners: "England and Russia are enfranchising women in wartime. . . . How long must women wait for liberty? . . . The government orders our banners destroyed because they tell the truth."

The promised arrests didn't take place until four o'clock in the afternoon, and they would be the first of many. Each batch of women received the identical sentence: thirty days in the Occoquan Workhouse. The presiding judge grew increasingly exasperated by the assembly line of women appearing before him almost daily. He said he didn't care to send "ladies of standing" to jail, and they could go free if they would promise to stop picketing, even though they were not charged with picketing, which was legal. The women greeted the offer with silence, which left the judge sputtering with frustration as he ordered the offenders to the workhouse.

There were two attempts made in the Senate to introduce bills that would prohibit picketing. Both efforts failed. Instead, there was a resolution introduced in the House calling for an investigation of the police for allowing mob attacks on the women. As public opinion began to shift toward the suffragists, government officials turned to harsher measures in a last desperate attempt to quash the protests. The suffragists braced for what they feared was ahead. Lucy Burns recalled what Warden Whittaker had said to her in July when she came to assist the picketers who had been pardoned by Wilson. "Now that you women are going away, I have something to say to you," Whittaker said, fixing an angry gaze on Burns, who he knew was one of the ringleaders. "The next lot of women who come here won't be treated with the same consideration that these women were."

Wilson had a war to fight, and suffrage was a distraction. On the afternoon of September 4, the president led his first call-up of drafted men in a parade down Pennsylvania Avenue. These "soldiers of freedom" were on their way to the battlefields of France. On the heels of the men came a thin line of women. Their golden banners fluttered in the late summer breeze with the plaintive question: "Mr. President, how long must women be denied a voice in a government which is conscripting their sons?" Thirteen women were arrested that afternoon and sentenced to sixty days at Occoquan, twice what the government had meted out just days before, and reflecting Wilson's determination to break the pickets through intimidation.

It didn't take long for word to reach the outside world about conditions at Occoquan. A prominent judge, whose daughter was imprisoned, urged his senator to visit the jail, and the lawmaker, a member of the Democratic leadership, came away horrified at the deteriorating health of the inmates. A prison matron who sympathized with the suffragists submitted an affidavit that said blankets were washed only once a year and that staples such as beans, hominy, rice, and cornmeal were infested with worms. She said the first suffragists took the worms that were floating in their soup and sent them to Warden Whittaker on a spoon. Later groups tried to make sport of the worms, holding contests among the tables on how many worms and weevils could be found. When one table ran up a score of fifteen, enthusiasm for the game plummeted, along with appetites. Suffragists who were impudent were put on a diet of bread and water. These revelations prompted Representative Jeannette Rankin of Montana, the only woman member of Congress, to introduce a resolution calling for an investigation of the workhouse.

As the summer of 1917 came to a close, Wilson was in a tight spot. The women used his own words about democracy against him and personalized the fight in a way he had not anticipated. On September 7, one of his dearest friends and political backers resigned as collector of the Port of New York to protest Wilson's handling of the suffrage issue. It was a body blow to the proud Wilson. Dudley Field Malone had campaigned for Wilson in the West, urging women to reelect the president on the promise that there would be a federal suffrage amendment. Instead there were mass arrests of women peacefully picketing followed by trumped-up charges and illegal jailing under unspeakable conditions. In a lengthy letter that was made public, Malone urged Wilson to put the full prestige of the presidency behind a suffrage amendment and submit it to Congress as a war measure. He noted that England and Russia, in the midst of the "Great War," as the European conflict was known, had assured women the vote. "I think it is high time that men in this generation, at some cost to themselves, stood up to battle for the national enfranchisement of American women."

The Malone resignation vindicated Paul's tactics. Even Carrie Chapman Catt, who condemned the picketing, applauded Malone's protest and his conclusion that it was the government that had behaved shamefully. A week later, on September 14, the chairman of the Senate Committee on Suffrage paid a surprise visit to the workhouse, and on the following day, filed a report that recommended the Senate pass the suffrage amendment. The House responded by creating its own Committee on Suffrage, by a vote of 181 to 107, denying, of course, that the pickets and the arrests had pressured them into acting. The Senate recommendation and the existence of the new House

Committee on Suffrage were breakthroughs, but no guar-
antees of prompt action. The lawmakers had the naive
impression that they had done enough by advancing this
far, and that the grateful suffragists would cease and desist.
They couldn't have been more mistaken.

Instead, the women took their protest inside the walls of
the workhouse, demanding to be treated as political prisoners. Lucy Burns, with her flaming red hair, athletic bearing, and fiery intellect, was the perfect leader for this next,
more dangerous phase of the campaign. She looked the
part and could handle the emotional and physical stress
better than almost anybody else. When the prison officials
picked up on her subversive activity, they quickly put her
into solitary. But removing the leader only intensified the
rebellion. A piece of paper outlining the rights of political
prisoners was passed through holes in the wall surrounding
lead pipes until it was signed by all the suffrage prisoners.
It said the women would do no work while in prison, and
that they demanded the right to consult an attorney,
unlimited visits by friends and family, reading and writing
materials, and food brought to them from the outside. It
was a historic document not only in the progress of suffrage but also because it was the first time any group had
organized to define the special status of political prisoners.

The prison officials didn't care about historical precedent. They responded by transferring every woman who
signed the paper along with their leader, Lucy Burns, to
the local District jail, where they were placed in solitary
confinement. Not only were their very reasonable demands
ignored, they were further punished and denied even the

modicum of decent treatment given common criminals. Alice Paul was still on the outside, organizing the public relations campaign. She didn't feel she had the luxury of being arrested. Her job was to make sure that every ugly detail of prison life got circulated for maximum shock effect. National Woman's Party speakers traveled the country telling the tales and tailoring their remarks for the audience. Democratic strongholds in the South rose up in disgust on hearing how white women were forced to sleep in the same dormitories with black women and even had to paint their toilet facilities. Southern men would vow to go to Washington "and burn that jail down." The warden got so many death threats that he had to carry a gun.

On October 6, the last day of Congress's emergency war session, there had been no further action on suffrage. Alice Paul led a contingent of eleven women to the White House gates to protest Wilson's allowing the lawmakers to go home without addressing suffrage. The women were arrested, and two days later faced trial. Asked if they wished to make a statement on their behalf, Paul rose and faced the judge. "We do not wish to make any plea before this court," she said calmly. "We do not consider ourselves subject to this court, since as an unenfranchised class we have nothing to do with the making of the laws which have put us in this position." Although the women were found guilty, the judge gave them a suspended sentence, which meant that they were free to leave. Either the authorities were afraid to mess with Paul, or this was yet another shift in the White House strategy. Paul didn't know which it was, but soon after, on October 20, she was back at the West Gate of the White House with a banner that carried the powerful message Wilson used to promote the second Liberty Bond loan of 1917: "The time has come to conquer or submit. For us there can be but one choice. We have made it."

A crowd gathered to watch as Paul and two other women were placed in a patrol wagon and taken to the District jail. "I am being imprisoned not because I obstructed traffic," Paul shouted for all to hear, "but because I pointed out to President Wilson the fact that he is obstructing the progress of justice and democracy at home while Americans fight for it abroad!" One of the women Paul was protesting with had a lover in Wilson's cabinet, who was privately pressing Wilson to yield on suffrage. Wilson's attitude was like that of many men of his era and social status. He didn't think women should be without the vote, but it wasn't a pressing priority. The high-level conduit, while useful, could not head off the confrontation, or spare the consequences to the women. Paul was sentenced to seven months in jail, the longest internment by far of any of the suffragists. The authorities no doubt thought that by removing the main instigator they would deprive the movement of its emotional energy, but once again they miscalculated. Arresting and confining Paul proved to be the climactic mistake of the Wilson administration.

It was late afternoon on October 20 when Paul and the others were admitted to the jail. They joined ten other suffragists who had been brought in four days earlier, who were packed in along with about seventy-five other women prisoners in three tiers of cells. The air smelled foul, and the windows, high above the cells, were shut tightly. The suffragists, on seeing Paul, immediately appealed to her as their leader to open a window and get them some fresh air. Paul noticed a rope attached to one small, round window high above her, and she asked the matron why the window hadn't been opened. "If we started opening windows, we should have to give the colored women more clothes," the matron told her.

Paul hadn't yet been locked in her cell, and before anybody could stop her, she pulled the window open. But she had no place to fasten the rope to hold it in place, so she just stood there with it, defying anybody to take it away. The matron called in the guards, and it took two of them to disarm Paul, who weighed all of ninety-five pounds. The tussle ended when the rope broke and the window closed. By one account, as the guards hustled Paul into her cell, she reached into the pocket of her coat, where she had secreted a copy of Elizabeth Browning's poems, and taking aim, tossed the volume at the faraway window, shattering the glass. That tale is almost too perfect and could be mythology. Another version has Paul instigating an attack on the windows by having the prisoners hurl their tin drinking cups at the panes until finally cracking through and letting in the outside air. Paul did contribute her book of poetry to the effort, and it was an exhilarating moment when the glass broke to allow in the cool October air.

The lack of privacy and the poor quality of food wore on the women. The guards would tear down the blankets the women hung on the bars of the cell in a feeble attempt to shield themselves from prying eyes. The food was almost always raw salt pork, some sort of liquid— either coffee or soup—bread, and occasionally molasses. Almost no one could eat the raw pork. One suffragist who managed to get it down would call out from her cell to advise the others to close their eyes and swallow the small pieces without chewing. Reflecting later on the experience, Paul said, "However gaily you start out in prison to keep up a rebellious protest, it is nevertheless a terribly difficult thing to do in the face of the constant cold and hunger of undernourishment. Bread and water, and occasional molasses, is not a diet destined to sustain rebellion long. And soon weakness overtook us."

After two weeks of this, without any exercise and never leaving their cells, all but seven of eighty prisoners were released. The remaining seven, including Paul, were allowed in the prison yard, but Paul was too weak to move from her bed. She and another woman, who had collapsed in the yard, were taken on stretchers that night to the prison hospital. There in the dark, as they lay in adjoining beds, the two women conspired to undertake a hunger strike, the ultimate form of protest left to them in their weakened state. The prison authorities alternately cajoled and threatened the women to get them to eat. The jail physician warned that they would be forcibly fed if they didn't cooperate. Others raised the prospect of moving them to St. Elizabeth's, a hospital for the insane, from where they might never emerge.

After their hunger strike had gone on for about three days, a Dr. White, who headed St. Elizabeth's, visited Paul in her cell at the jail. "Please talk," he said to her in a kindly way. "Tell me about suffrage; why you have opposed the president; the whole history of your campaign; why you picket; what you hope to accomplish by it. Just talk freely."

"Indeed I'll talk," Paul said gaily, welcoming the chance to get on her soapbox. It didn't occur to her that the purpose of these questions was to probe her sanity. She sat upright in bed and talked at length while Dr. White listened attentively and a stenographer took down everything she said. She recalled later that it was one of the best speeches she'd ever made. She covered everything from the long history of the suffrage struggle to the political theory of protest and the status of the amendment on Capitol Hill. When Dr. White interrupted at one point to ask whether President Wilson had mistreated the suffragists, Paul offered what amounted to a dissertation on Wilson's power as the leader of his party and the country to set the agenda. Singling him out was not personal, she said, it was because he was the president.

Her answer did not satisfy the doctor. "But isn't President Wilson directly responsible for the abuses and indignities which have been heaped upon you? You are suffering now as a result of his brutality, are you not?" Paul said it was impossible to know the extent of Wilson's knowledge about the plight of the women currently in prison, although he had sanctioned the early arrests. Still, Paul had no idea where this was leading until White shone a small light into her eyes and it dawned on her that he was there to examine her, not to learn about suffrage. Still, she continued to prattle on, unwittingly providing him with the ammunition he needed to make the case that she had an unhealthy obsession about President Wilson. White returned the following day accompanied by another psychiatrist and various prison authorities. They asked Paul to repeat many of the things she had said, which she did. And they promised that if she stopped her hunger strike, there would be an immediate investigation into the horrific conditions in the jail that she had experienced.

"Will you consent to treat the suffragists as political prisoners?" Paul asked. That would have been a deal worth striking. But the answer was no, so Paul said she would not abandon her hunger strike. She heard the order given to forcibly feed her, and she was immediately taken on a stretcher into the psychopathic ward of the prison hospital and put into isolation. A nurse came by every hour to "observe" her and to shine a light in her face, making sleep all but impossible. This was where prisoners waiting to be transferred to a mental institution awaited their commitment papers. The nurses explained to Paul that all it took to commit a prisoner to St. Elizabeth's was an order signed by two examining psychiatrists. She began to think that this was the plan for her when the jail doctor ordered the forcible feeding to begin.

Paul and another woman, Rose Winslow, were the first suffragists to be fed forcibly, a procedure they underwent three times a day. Winslow, a Polish immigrant who represented women workers, scribbled notes on little scraps of paper about what was going on and smuggled them out to her husband. She revealed that Paul was in the psychopathic ward, and she exposed the graphic details of having a pipe shoved down into your stomach, the vomiting that occurs, and the painful irritation. "Never was there a sentence like ours for such an offense as ours, even in England," she wrote. "No woman ever got it over there even for tearing down buildings. And during all that agitation, we were busy saying that never would such things happen in the United States. . . . All the officers here know we are making this hunger strike so that women fighting for liberty may be considered political prisoners; we have told them. God knows we don't want other women ever to have to do this over again." Lucy Burns sent out messages to the suffrage community documenting Paul's ordeal and asking women to send a telegram to President Wilson demanding her release. The head of the Massachusetts antisuffrage movement wired back: She should stay there.

The hunger strike spread to other prisoners in the jail and at the workhouse, competing with war news on the front page. Paul's confinement stunned the nation as word got out that she was being kept incommunicado in a ward for mental patients and forcibly fed. On the late afternoon of November 10, 1917, forty-one women from sixteen states lined up in front of the White House with their gold-lettered banners and suffrage flags to protest the unspeakable treatment of their leader. It was the longest single picket line of the campaign. The women were promptly arrested, judged guilty, and sent home. They were not sentenced. There was no more room in the jail or the workhouse, and the administration feared the political fallout of incarcerating such a large group of Paul's ardent followers all at once. But the women would not be so easily deterred. They returned the next day to the White House to resume picketing, and once again they were arrested. This time they were told the judge wasn't ready to hear their case. Back to the White House they marched, where they were arrested a third time.

Now the game was over, and the judge handed out sentences that ranged from six days to six months. Lucy Burns got the maximum; Mrs. Mary Nolan, seventy-three, received the lightest sentence, in deference to her age. The judge warned the elderly woman that prison could damage her health and even bring death and urged that she pay the fine instead. Mrs. Nolan, who was frail and small and walked with a limp, drew herself up as tall as she could and said that she had a nephew fighting for democracy in France, offering his life for his country. "I should be ashamed if I did not join these brave women in their fight for democracy in America. I should be proud of the honor to die in prison for the liberty of American women."

All but one of the forty-one women were sent to Occoquan, where they ran directly into the buzz saw of Warden Whittaker. He had had his fill of suffragists and didn't want to hear their demand to be treated as political prisoners. The women had agreed that Mrs. Lawrence Lewis of Philadelphia would speak for them. She had barely said anything when Whittaker told her to shut up and ordered two of his prison goons to take her away. That was the beginning of what would be remembered in suffrage annals as the "Night of Terror." The other women were hauled off with brutal force and confined to dark stone *such hostility*

cells that were filthy and had no window except for a tiny sliver at the top. Mrs. Nolan remembered pleading with the guard who dragged her to her cell to take care with her lame foot, but he ignored her. "I was jerked down the steps and away into the dark," she said. "I didn't have my feet on the ground. I guess that saved me."

The guards, given free rein, indulged their pent-up hostility against the women. Mrs. Nolan reported one of the men yelling, "Damned Suffrager! My mother ain't no Suffrager! I will put you through hell!" When a guard tossed Mrs. Lewis into her cell, her head struck the iron bed, and she was knocked to the floor, unconscious. Another woman whose head hit the wall was up all night and desperately ill, having suffered a heart attack. The women begged for medical attention, but it was refused. Whittaker told them to be quiet or he would put them in straitjackets with a brace and bit in their mouths. Lucy Burns, deposited in a nearby cell, heard the commotion and began to call the roll. In a melodious voice that belied the horror around her, she sang out one name after another. The guards told her to shut up, but she kept on calling the roll. Finally the guards handcuffed her and then attached the handcuffs above her head to the cell door, rendering her immobile. She was left that way all night. The woman in the cell directly across from Burns, in a show of solidarity, put her hands above her head and stood in the same position.

After the women had refused food for three days, the prison officials tried to tempt them with fried chicken and salad, four-star cuisine compared to the usual prison fare.

Burns passed a note to the others that said, "I think this riotous feast which has just passed our doors is the last effort of the institution to dislodge all of us who can be dislodged. They think there is nothing in our souls above fried chicken."

By the seventh day, Whittaker began to fear for the lives of his prisoners and how that might affect his career and reputation. In an attempt to break the hunger strike, he ordered Burns and Lewis, the two leaders, moved to the jail in Washington where Alice Paul was confined. He also ordered that the two women be forcibly fed, a gruesome experience that Burns described on scraps of paper she smuggled out of the jail. It took five people to hold her down, and when she refused to open her mouth, they shoved the feeding tube up her nostril, which is extremely painful and causes a copious nosebleed. She said the food sank in her stomach like a ball of lead, and the procedure left her feeling quite ill.

Isolated from their leaders, the rest of the women were told that the hunger strike was over and the other suffragists had resumed prison work. They suspected these were lies, and did not yield. They also were told that their demand to be treated as political prisoners had no merit and that their lawyer had been called off the case. Actually, a lawyer for the National Woman's Party had attempted to gain access to Occoquan immediately after their detention, but he was refused. A detachment of U.S. Marines guarded the workhouse, and when one of the marines brought back tales of unspeakable tortures, the attorney was able to get a court order to force his way into the prison. What he found was a group of women in such a weakened state that he had to move quickly. He decided to seek a writ of habeas corpus to force the government to bring the prisoners into court and show cause why, since the women had been arrested for acts committed in the District of Columbia, they were serving time in "alien territory," namely Virginia. It was admittedly a ploy, but a good one.

The nightmare scenario for the government was exposing the treatment of the suffragists, which would inevitably come out in any court proceeding. It took six tries before a deputy marshal was able to serve the suddenly elusive Warden Whittaker with the writ, compelling him to produce the suffrage prisoners in court in Alexandria, Virginia, on November 23. Confronted with the court order, Whittaker erupted in violent anger and threatened various reprisals, which he would be in no position to carry out. When the trial got under way, Whittaker was there, dressed in his Sunday best, along with an array of government officials and a small army of newspaper reporters. With the exception of Whittaker, who knew what to expect, everybody present registered visible shock when the suffragists filed into the courtroom. Appearing haggard and sick, some were so weak that they couldn't sit through the proceedings and had to lie down on the wooden benches. Some still bore dark bruises from the Night of Terror. Most had trouble focusing and seemed in a daze.

Surveying the human wreckage, the judge took almost no time to rule that the women had been illegally taken to the workhouse. He ordered them transferred to the

District jail, where they would join Alice Paul and Rose Winslow, adding the strength of their numbers to the two women's ongoing hunger strike. Released into the custody of their lawyer until the transfer could take place, the women spent the evening at National Woman's Party headquarters, where they broke their fast, sipping hot milk. The next morning, back in jail, they resumed their hunger strike. Faced with thirty women ready to risk their health and even their lives, with eight already near physical collapse, the White House did a quick assessment. They obviously couldn't let the women starve to death, yet there were social and political consequences to force feeding such a large group. Either way, they weren't likely to break the women's will and determination. It was time to concede defeat. The administration ordered the doors of the jail thrown open and all suffrage prisoners released without condition on November 27 and 28.

7

Out of Bondage

Every seat was taken on December 4 at Washington's Belasco Theatre for a ceremony honoring the eighty-one women who had served time in the jail or the workhouse. An overflow crowd of four thousand stood outside in the bitter cold to pay their respects. Each prison suffragist received a tiny silver replica of a prison cell door with a heart-shaped lock. When Paul stepped to the stage, the applause reached a crescendo and continued until she left the platform. The inhumane conditions that the suffragists exposed won sympathy for their cause and also indebted them to the prison population. The regular prisoners called these angels of activism "the strange ladies," and for months afterward appealed to them for help. When they wondered if staging a hunger strike could improve their situation the way it had for the suffragists, the women told them no, that without an organization to back them, they were at the mercy of the authorities. The suffragists filed damage suits amounting to $800,000 against Whittaker and other prison officials in a symbolic attempt to hold the government responsible for the brutality.

The Belasco mass meeting had a revivalist flavor and raised $83,326 for the National Woman's Party. Mrs. Alva Belmont opened the evening with a testimonial to the months of picketing that had finally gotten the government's attention. Belmont was an acolyte of the Pankhursts and was the first American suffragist leader to urge the militancy that Paul then carried out. It was at Belmont's home that Paul and Lucy Burns first unveiled their plan to hold the Democratic Party responsible for blocking suffrage. Belmont was one of a handful of wealthy women who funded the suffrage movement. Her previous husband had been a Vanderbilt, and when she caught him cheating on her, she sued for divorce, which at the time was permitted to be initiated by a woman in only three states. She was awarded a generous settlement, and a year later married the man she had been having an affair with while married to Vanderbilt. Oliver Belmont died after a few years, and by the time she inherited his estate, her transformation from socialite to suffragist was so complete that her influence rivaled that of Paul's in running the National Woman's Party.

Congress reconvened on December 4, and President Wilson delivered a message that underscored America's commitment to the Great War and urged passage of several measures he needed as commander in chief. There was not a word about suffrage, which the suffragists found disappointing, but Congress nevertheless began to take action. The chairman of the House Committee on Suffrage, who had previously predicted the House wouldn't pass the amendment before 1920, set the date of January 10, 1918, for a vote. The debate was long and contentious as member after member rose to exhort his colleagues along with the press corps and an unusually large crowd of spectators. Suffragists arriving in the morning and sitting in the gallery had brought their lunch, anticipating a long wait before the tally. Not until evening, when Representative James Robert Mann of Illinois, a suffrage supporter, was brought in from his hospital bed to cast his vote, did Paul and the other leaders begin to relax. Mann was so ill that he hadn't received any visitors other than his wife and secretary for six months, yet he managed to make the vote.

Opponents of suffrage castigated the women for their tactics. Representative William Gordon of Ohio, a Democrat, decried the "women militants" who spent the summer and fall "coaxing, teasing, and nagging the President of the United States for the purpose of inducing him, by coercion, to club Congress into adopting this joint resolution." The congressman's comments elicited cries and jeers from both sides in the debate. "They got him!" shouted the spectators. Other lawmakers felt compelled to minimize the impact of the picketing, even as they supported suffrage. "I do not approve of anything unwomanly anywhere, anytime, and my course today in supporting this suffrage amendment is not guided by such conduct on the part of a very few women here or elsewhere," insisted Oklahoma Democrat Scott Ferris.

The women didn't know until the vote was taken how much pressure Wilson had applied behind the scenes. By Paul's count, Wilson saved the day, commandeering 6 votes that had eluded the suffragists. The House passed the suffrage amendment on January 10, 1918, by a vote of 274 to 136, the required two-thirds majority plus 1 vote to spare. One congressman left his hospital bed and had to be helped into the House chamber to cast his vote for suffrage. Another put off having a broken arm treated, preferring to withstand the physical pain rather than miss the vote. It was exactly forty years to the day from when the amendment was first introduced in Congress, and exactly one year to the day since the first picket carrying a suffrage banner stood at the White House gate. It was an exhilarating moment, but one that would mean nothing if the women couldn't get the votes in the Senate, where they were 11 votes short.

Wilson's show of strength had worked in the House, and the women hoped he would show the same commitment on the Senate side. All picketing was halted in deference to the new alliance with the White House, and there was a period of calm as the women worked to lobby senators, methodically picking up votes one by one. The Senate then had 96 members, 2 from each of the 48 states. A two-thirds majority to pass an amendment meant that the women needed 64 votes. They counted 53 pledges of support and 43 opponents, which meant they must turn 11 noes into yeses. Former president Theodore Roosevelt was a valuable ally in persuading the few unconvinced Republican senators that their party held the high ground on suffrage and that they should support it. Former president William Howard Taft proved his limited intellect and tone-deaf politics when he refused to support any proposition that added more voters to the rolls. "Why, I'd take the vote away from most of the men," he declared. Herbert Hoover, who was Wilson's chief food administrator and would later be elected president, dodged the issue and was the only man prominent in public life who refused even to see a suffrage representative. Later, when he announced his candidacy for the Republican nomination for president, he had his secretary write a letter saying he had always supported suffrage.

Paul developed a card index that kept tabs on every member, from his golf partners and drinking habits to whether his mother or his wife had more influence over him. "Mothers continue to have strong influence over their sons," Maud Younger explained to the *New York Times* in a March 1919 interview. "Some married men listen to their mothers more than to their wives. You will hear a man telling his wife how his mother used to do it, and then we know . . . if we can make of her a strong advocate for suffrage we have the best of chances of winning the son. Or if it is the wife who has the strong influence and she is an anti, we know that our first work must be to convert the wife to our cause." By knowing a senator's professional and personal quirks, the women could uncover vulnerabilities. There was even a card entry for ancestry. "Some races are more disposed to suffrage than others," Younger said.

When Paul first started out in 1913, the money allotted for lobbying by the woman's movement was $10. By

1919, Paul's expenses in Washington were $100,000. There were so many women canvassing Capitol Hill that one congressman was heard to complain, "This place looks like a millinery establishment." Paul's "Three Pressure System" went after each potential vote directly with lobbyist visits; then with a "Political Committee" charged with bringing in prominent people to exert pressure; and finally through an "Organization and Legislative Committee" that gathered support in the senator's home state for what today we call grassroots lobbying. Paul called the card index "our thermometer," and when it showed there was no hope of reaching a senator by direct action—that is, an appeal to reason and political rationale by a suffrage lobbyist—she would trigger the other pressure points.

Paul's lobbying effort won over, however grudgingly, some of the more hard-shelled opponents, and the women were only two votes short when the chairman of the Committee on Suffrage announced he would take up the amendment on May 10. "The best of the men politicians had to concede that Paul played their game with extraordinary success," reported the *New York Times*. "She gave those members of Congress who had their ears to the ground their own medicine, fortified to a new degree and in such a way that they hardly knew what was happening to them."

The galleries were packed on May 10 when Committee on Suffrage chairman Andreus Aristides Jones of New Mexico rose and announced that he would not call up the amendment that day. He set a new date: June 27. Watching the surprise development, Maud Younger knew Jones as a placid, unhurried man who did not act on impulse. The suffrage side didn't have the votes, and Jones was buying them time. A sincere supporter of suffrage, he was one of the fathers of the amendment, although Younger points out that compared to mothers, "A father is so casual, especially when his child is an amendment to the Constitution."

Over the next six weeks the women tried to nail down the last votes. The holdouts rebelled at the "nagging" by "professional agitators," but on June 27, as the galleries filled again with spectators, the women were confident that victory was at hand. The White House had extracted a commitment from antisuffrage Democrat Senator Ollie M. James of Kentucky, unable to make the vote, that he would not ask a prosuffrage senator to refrain from voting to compensate for his enforced absence. Under Senate rules then, a two-thirds vote of those present would pass the amendment. Several foes were absent, which meant that the amendment would pass if no special provision was made.

Then a suffrage opponent rose to read a telegram from the hospitalized Senator James, imploring the committee to uphold his rights and pair him with a suffrage supporter. Soon, a full-blown filibuster was under way. Suffrage opponents were prepared to hold the floor for weeks, and the military budget had to be passed before July 1 or the army would run out of money. It was tantamount to a gun held to the head, and Chairman Jones knew it. He withdrew his motion to consider the suffrage amendment. The antisuffrage side was triumphant. "Suffrage is dead for this session," announced Tennessee Senator Kenneth D.

nagging —
do they
call lobbying
by men
nagging?

McKellar. "The senators don't like being nagged anymore. They are tired of it."

The Senate was about to recess for the summer, and the Democrats had given the women no assurances about when suffrage might again be considered. Paul told the *New York Times* in a rare interview, "Whenever we picketed the White House, we noticed the president became more active in our cause, and whenever we let up there was a relaxation." It was time to resume the protests. The women chose August 6, 1918, the anniversary of the birth of Inez Milholland Boissevain. Almost a hundred women dressed in white met at the base of the Lafayette monument in the park directly opposite the White House. They held banners of purple, white, and gold, but one stood out above the others with Boissevain's last words, "Mr. President, how much longer must women wait for liberty?" As the first speaker began, she was seized by a policeman and placed under arrest. One after another, as the speakers took their place, they were taken away to waiting patrol cars. An audience of onlookers watched in amazement as a total of forty-eight women were roughed up and hauled off, their banners streaming from the backs of the paddy wagons. Alice Paul and Lucy Burns were among them.

The women were told that the police arrested them under the orders of President Wilson's military aide. They were charged with climbing a statue and holding a meeting on public grounds, charges more spurious even than obstructing traffic. All were released on bail and ordered to appear in court the next day, but the government's attorney was so perplexed that he put off the trial for ten days to ponder "what offense, if any" the women could legitimately be charged with.

On the day of the trial, Alice Paul spoke for the group. She said: "As a disenfranchised class we feel that we are not subject to the jurisdiction of this court and therefore refuse to take any part in its proceedings. We also feel that we have done nothing to justify our being brought before it." Then she and the others sat down and refused to respond to any questions, flummoxing the judge, who called a fifteen-minute recess to consider bringing contempt charges. In the end, the judge settled on relatively light sentences of $5 or $10 fines and ten or fifteen days in prison. The shorter sentences were designed to head off any extended hunger strikes, which was prudent. But then the administration made another incalculable error. Rather than send the women back to the jail or the workhouse, they opened a separate building that had previously been used as a men's workhouse but that had been condemned during the Roosevelt administration. Unfit for human habitation, the building had stood empty since 1909.

The twenty-six suffragists assigned to the dank building were there because they attempted to hold a meeting in a public park. It was hardly the kind of offense to warrant such dismal surroundings. The cells were damp and cold, with only a small grating to allow a little light to get through. The building had been vacant for so long that the air didn't move, the stench was unbearable, and the water made the women sick, perhaps because the pipes hadn't been used for so long. Desperate for relief from the

foul odors in the cells, the women took the straw pallets
they were issued for beds and lay down on the stone floor
of the jail, ignoring orders to return to their cells. The
physical conditions were the worst that the suffragists had
encountered, and it didn't take long for word to get out
around the country, and for visitors, including a stream of
prominent senators, to lodge protests with the administration. After five days the women were released, some so
sickened by the drinking water and the constant cold that
they could barely make it to a waiting ambulance.

Photographs of white-haired suffragists being helped
from jail along with testimonials from prominent politicians prompted the Republicans in the Senate for the first
time to take a position as a party in favor of forcing suffrage to a vote. There was a political calculation as well.
The congressional elections of 1918 were approaching,
and the Republicans, the minority party in Congress,
hoped a prosuffrage stand would give them an advantage
and perhaps vault them into the majority. The Democrats
continued to toy with suffrage, giving it lip service but
refusing to take the necessary steps to ensure passage of
the amendment. The women kept up their protests at the
Lafayette monument. Many were arrested and then immediately released before the authorities tired of the revolving
door and gave Paul a permit to conduct suffrage demonstrations in Lafayette Park.

While Paul was happy to see an end to the police harassment, she also knew that peaceably assembling in the park
wouldn't change anything in the Senate. She set the date
of September 16 for another mass demonstration at the

base of the Lafayette monument. The French general the marquis de Lafayette fought with the Americans against the British, and symbolized an alliance for liberty that President Wilson often invoked. But Wilson's encomiums to democracy and liberty had proved little more than empty words as he did little to advance the cause of suffrage. When Wilson learned that the women planned a four-o'clock demonstration, he announced that he would receive a delegation of suffragists from the West and the South on the same day at two o'clock. He told the women he was "heartily in sympathy" with them and would do all he could to promote an early vote for suffrage. Even if they were inclined to believe him, they knew better. Earlier in the day, the ranking Democrats in Congress had told the women to forget about it, that suffrage was "not on the program," and that the Committee on Suffrage would not convene.

Paul had been looking for a way to escalate the demonstrations, and now she had her answer. The women took the very words that Wilson had spoken to them that afternoon, and at the base of the Lafayette monument, they set them afire with a torch. This was the first time the president's words were burned, and the daring act thrilled the crowd that had gathered. Someone passed forward a $20 bill, and soon the suffragists were going through the crowd collecting donations. Many of the police on duty dug into their pockets to contribute. Wilson, heading out for his afternoon drive, had his driver turn the car so he didn't go out his usual gate, where he could see the hubbub. But he heard enough from news reports to know that it was trouble.

The next day, the chairman of the Senate Committee on Suffrage said he would bring forward the amendment and keep it before the Senate until there was a vote. Fewer than twenty-four hours earlier, he had declared suffrage dead for that session of Congress. The Democrats' reversal was the fastest response to any of Paul's protests.

Confident that they had gotten Wilson's attention, the National Woman's Party halted all demonstrations. Wearying of all the petitions, parades, and protests, the women were ready to cease and desist. The Senate debate opened on September 26, continued for five days, and culminated in a dramatic appearance by Wilson, normally a buttoned-up public speaker, who gave an emotional speech tying suffrage to America's ability to wage the Great War for humanity in Europe. "It is my duty to win the war and to ask you to remove every obstacle that stands in the way of winning it," he said, linking suffrage to patriotism in a way he had never done before. Wilson's moving and apparently heartfelt appeal was not enough, however, to melt the opposition. One antisuffrage Republican who refused to budge said the vote belonged only to the sex that fights and dies on the battlefield. Another senator voiced his opposition in a more jocular vein, saying he believed women superior to men, and that's why he didn't trust women with the vote.

When the roll call was taken, suffrage lost by two votes. It was an extraordinary snub of a wartime president.

Using parliamentary legerdemain, Chairman Jones managed to keep suffrage on the Senate calendar, which gave the suffrage side time to find two more votes. The

November congressional elections were just a month away, and the National Woman's Party plunged in with the goal of electing prosuffrage candidates. Senate contests in New Jersey and New Hampshire were between prosuffrage Democrats and antisuffrage Republicans, so the women asked Wilson to intervene, a natural enough request, since Wilson was a Democrat. But Wilson, preoccupied with the war, let the matter slide and didn't do anything for two weeks. Turning up the heat, the National Woman's Party went west and campaigned against Democrats and for Republicans in the prosuffrage states. It didn't matter to Alice Paul which party prevailed; they were all suffragists. But it meant a lot to Wilson, who didn't want to lose his Democratic majority in the Senate. Wilson got active at the eleventh hour, but by then it was too late. Republicans swept five of seven senatorial contests in the western states along with New Jersey and New Hampshire, enough to give them majority control in the next Congress.

On Capitol Hill, the women had resumed picketing in the weeks leading up to the election. The Capitol police would arrest them as soon as they appeared on the Capitol steps, confiscate their banners, and hold them for fifteen minutes in a basement guardroom before releasing them. As Election Day 1918 neared, and in the weeks immediately after, the standoff escalated. The women were roughed up as they were taken away and held until late afternoon, when the Senate was no longer in session. Outraged at being repeatedly arrested but never charged, the women took to wearing black armbands to signify the death of justice.

The irony of American women going to jail over the right

to vote while German women celebrated their newfound liberation was never greater than when the war ended. "We are all free voters of a free republic now," the women of Germany said in a message conveyed to the women of the United States by Jane Addams, a hero in Europe for her work establishing settlement houses for immigrants at the turn of the century. A social reformer and peace activist, Addams promoted the idea that women could clean up politics if they got the vote. "Politics is housekeeping on a grand scale," she said. German women got the vote in 1919, the year after the war ended. The German autocracy had collapsed, the kaiser had fled for his life, and America was rejoicing over its role in bringing democracy to Germany. The Great War had ended. Armistice Day was November 11, 1918. Despite the carnage—10 million men died throughout Europe—Wilson must have been feeling pretty good when he drafted his message for the opening of a special session of Congress on December 2. Unbidden, he included suffrage in his remarks, citing the war service of women as evidence that they were the equals of men in the factories and on the farms. "The least tribute we can pay them is to make them the equals of men in political rights," he concluded.

This was the first time since Wilson took office in 1913 that he deigned to mention suffrage at the opening of a congressional session. It was big news, but what would he do to turn his words into action? Apparently nothing because ten days later, Wilson sailed to France. The armistice, signed by more than thirty nations, ended the war but left the details of peace to be worked out at the

Paris Peace Conference. Wilson left behind no strategy to advance suffrage, and the Democrats who controlled this lame-duck session showed no inclination to do anything about securing the two needed votes without Wilson leading the way. On the list of things Wilson cared about, suffrage was once again near the bottom. Horrified by the slaughter of the war, he wanted to put in place a mechanism that could mediate conflicts and avoid future wars. He hoped to get European backing for his visionary idea for a League of Nations.

Edith accompanied her husband on the trip. Never before had a first lady traveled abroad. The all-male delegates to the peace conference did not permit a woman in their midst, so Edith stood behind a curtain for five hours listening to Wilson present his proposal, along with the debate that followed. World War I had been a clash of empires, and the delegates were more interested in divvying up the spoils and imposing reparations on the vanquished than conjuring up some Utopian scheme for the future.

If Wilson were a practical man, he would have realized he was on a fool's errand. Instead, caught up in his peace mission, he failed to see or appreciate the crisis of confidence in his leadership that was building back in Washington. It was late afternoon on December 16 when hundreds of women walked slowly in single file to Lafayette's statue, some carrying lighted torches, others the familiar purple, white, and gold banners. A Grecian urn placed at the base of the statue was set ablaze as Vida Milholland sang the "Marseillaise," the French freedom anthem the women had adopted as their cry for liberty. Silence fell over the crowd as an elderly woman approached the urn and tossed into the flames a copy of the speech Wilson had delivered upon arriving in France. "I have fought for liberty for seventeen years, and I protest against the President's leaving our country with this old fight here unwon," declared the Reverend Olympia Brown, eighty-four, of Wisconsin, one of the country's first ordained women ministers and a friend of Susan B. Anthony. Nineteen speakers in all consigned Wilson's various speeches extolling liberty and democracy to the bonfire.

The resulting spectacle made news around the world but elicited no response from Wilson. Alice Paul spent Christmas 1918 in bed, ostensibly resting but really devising a new plan of action. The urn was an attention-grabber; they would move it to the sidewalk in front of the White House and keep a fire burning until Congress passed the Susan B. Anthony amendment. The first watch fire of freedom was lit on New Year's Day 1919 with wood from a tree in Independence Square in Philadelphia. Women holding suffrage banners stood guard over the fire, and a bell hung in the balcony at the National Woman's Party headquarters across the park rang out each time Wilson's words were consumed by the flames. There was intermittent harassment—everything from the police trying to extinguish the fire to young men trying to smash the urn—but Paul and the others kept rekindling a new fire.

After four days and four nights, orders went out to arrest the women. Someone unearthed an old statute that banned the building of fires in public places between sunset and sunrise. Judged guilty, the women were sentenced to a $5 fine or five days in jail. The judge offered probation if they would promise not to set any more fires. The women, of course, chose jail, and immediately went on a hunger strike. And so the merry-go-round began again, with the women protesting, going to jail, and watch fires continuing to burn outside the White House. On January 13, the day the peace conference opened in Paris with Wilson playing a leading role, the police arrested twenty-three women who had been tending the fire outside the absentee president's front gate.

Wilson had been out of the country since mid-December. Not a day passed without front-page coverage of the arrests, along with the apparent determination of the suffragists to keep returning to the front lines whatever the punishment. Wilson could no longer ignore his home front, and began cabling Democratic leaders in the Senate to schedule a suffrage vote and bring the turmoil in front of the White House to an end. With Wilson active in the debate, Chairman Jones of the Committee on Suffrage announced that the Senate would take up the amendment on February 10. During a preliminary meeting among Democrats, South Carolina senator William P. Pollock, yielding to a cable he had received from Wilson, announced that he would vote for suffrage after months of waffling on the issue.

That left the suffrage side just one vote shy of victory. The Democrats brought in William Jennings Bryan, Wilson's former secretary of state and a compelling orator, in an eleventh-hour effort to turn the last vote. Bryan argued politics. Suffrage is coming, he said, "in spite of, if not with the aid of the Democratic Party." Failure to pass suffrage would burden Democrats with the charge that they prevented its passage.

On February 9, the day before the vote, the women burned Wilson in effigy. It was only a paper figure—a cartoon, really—but the act was highly suggestive and symbolic. The police moved in, scooping up dozens of suffragists and hauling them away in patrol cars. No sooner did the police clear the sidewalk than fresh reinforcements of women and banners and kindling wood arrived from headquarters. Faced with an unending stream of women willing to go to jail, the police declared the area a military zone, forbidding anybody to enter or leave, freezing into place a representative band of women to parade up and down a small section of sidewalk.

When the roll was called on February 10, the amendment lost by one vote. The yes votes were divided between the parties—thirty-two Republicans, thirty-one Democrats. Twenty-one Democrats and twelve Republicans voted "no." The results confirmed Paul's analysis that the blame belonged squarely on the party in power and a president who performed only when pushed and prodded, and who did too little too late. A few blocks away, at the District courthouse, thirty-nine women who had been arrested the previous day were being tried. After sentencing twenty-six of them to jail, the judge asked how many were left. Told that a third of the women remained, the judge threw up his hands and arbitrarily dismissed the last thirteen cases. He was weary of the charade.

A railroad car dubbed the "Prison Special" toured the

country with women who had served time in jail. These "prison specialists," outfitted in prison garb, spoke to packed houses everywhere, winning friends for suffrage and arousing thousands, especially in the South, to condemn the administration's shameful treatment of women and to bombard the White House with cables of dismay.

Wilson was due to return on February 24, docking in Boston. The newspapers were filled with details of the elaborate welcome ceremony being planned. The focus was on Wilson's triumphs abroad; there was no mention of the unfinished business of suffrage. Alice Paul decided to travel to Boston to arrange a demonstration. She didn't hide what she was doing. On the contrary, she put out a press release detailing her plans. A line of silent sentinels would greet the president holding banners with the familiar suffrage slogan "Mr. President, how much longer must women wait for liberty?" In addition, a large banner made especially for the occasion would remind Wilson of what he told the Senate on September 20: "We shall not only be distrusted but we shall deserve to be distrusted if we do not enfranchise women." The large printed banner concluded with a direct appeal to Wilson: "You alone can remove this distrust by securing the one vote needed to pass the suffrage amendment before March 4."

The police didn't want the women getting anywhere near Wilson. They established a line in front of the reviewing stand beyond which no suffrage demonstrator was permitted. Marines guarded the line. The twenty-two women Paul had recruited for the day managed to weave their way into the forbidden area until they stood at the base of the reviewing stand, staring straight at the marines who were supposed to block their way. They were there about forty-five minutes before the local police chief politely asked them to move until Wilson had gone by. The women refused. Patrol wagons were on the scene within minutes, and the women were taken off. The whole operation didn't take long, and the police, hoping to avoid a scene, treated the women with such deference, it was as though they were handling human dynamite. Indeed, it was an explosive situation. No matter how gingerly the police approached their task, the sight of these women being loaded into paddy wagons excited the citizens of Boston far more than anything Wilson later said in his speech.

Wilson didn't witness any of the commotion, but his carriage did drive by the National Woman's Party headquarters in Boston. When he saw the purple, white, and gold signature colors of the suffrage movement, the smile faded from his face and he looked the other way. On his lap and visible from the street was a morning newspaper with a large, boldface headline about the upcoming demonstration.

The women were taken to Boston's House of Detention, a loathsome place under the courthouse where they spent the night sleeping four to a cell until they could be arraigned. They were charged with "loitering more than seven minutes." The following morning the women were taken to the second floor of the courthouse and told that the proceedings would be closed to the public. Since every American citizen has the right to a public trial, the women refused to give their correct names; many presented themselves as Jane Doe. Sixteen of the women were taken to the Charles Street Jail, where their living conditions were widely publicized by the Boston newspapers. Telegrams of protest poured into the city from around the country, and the jail's "bucket system" became infamous. Each cell was assigned two wooden buckets of water, one for bathing and the other for a toilet, which the prisoners emptied when permitted into the yard at most once a day.

The country was in high dudgeon over the coarse treatment of the ladies when a mysterious benefactor appeared to pay fines that in fact had never been levied. The man gave his name as E. J. Howe, and thanks to his largesse, the women were released two at a time over the next few days. Howe said he was acting on behalf of a client that he would not identify, and once he'd made the payments, he vanished, and reporters were never able to track him down to question him further. It was speculated that his so-called client was the city of Boston, desperate to get out of the spotlight and end the embarrassment created by jailing the suffragists.

When Wilson arrived back in Washington, one of the first things he did was visit the Capitol and meet with the Democratic chairman of the Committee on Suffrage, Senator Jones of New Mexico. Having suffered a humiliating defeat on suffrage just weeks earlier, Jones didn't want to risk bringing up the measure again. But with the Republicans poised to take control of the next session of Congress, Wilson persuaded Jones that if Democrats wanted credit for passing the federal amendment, they had to act before the Republicans were in the majority. To get around a procedural prohibition against rehearing a measure that's already been considered, Jones reworded the amendment to give the states the power to enforce woman suffrage, with the federal government stepping in only if the states failed to comply. This nod to states' rights won over Louisiana senator Edward Gay, giving the suffrage side the sixty-four votes needed. Democrats had the votes, but the Republican leadership didn't want to give the opposition a political victory, so they prevented the amendment from coming to a vote. The new Republican Congress would not convene until December, nine months away, unless Wilson called a special emergency session sooner.

With the close of Congress, Wilson immediately left for Europe. On his way to set sail, he stopped in New York to address a peace rally at the Metropolitan Opera House for his proposed League of Nations. Paul was waiting. She had arranged a demonstration outside the opera house with the purpose of pressuring Wilson into calling an early session of Congress. When the picket line of twenty-five women neared the building on the clear and chilly evening of March 4, two hundred policemen barreled into them, clubs swinging, repelling and trampling the women. "The women fought like catamounts," reported the *New York Times* in a front-page dispatch the next morning. But they were "no match" for the policemen, who descended on them along with soldiers, sailors, and civilians who joined in the melee. "Forty or more women who paraded last night came away with black eyes, broken lips and bruised cheeks," the story said.

Six women were arrested and taken to a police station, Paul among them. The women went on a silence strike, offering only the name Jane Doe. Charged with disorderly conduct and interfering with the police, they were locked in separate cells awaiting trial. They anticipated being detained at least overnight when half an hour later, the order came to release them. With Paul leading the charge, they headed straight back to the demonstration site. The *Times* account refers to "a mysterious stenographer" within the opera house. Somebody was taking notes on Wilson's speech, and with stunning speed, the suffragists were translating the steno notes into typewritten pages and relaying them to the demonstrators. On Fortieth Street between Broadway and Sixth Avenue, Elsie Hill, a teacher of French from Connecticut and the daughter of a former congressman, struck a match to the first sheets of the speech. Paul and the other freed suffragists tossed more pages on the bonfire, and as the flames became visible above the crowd, a double line of patrolmen raced to the scene, and a second bloody encounter was under way.

This was a superheated patriotic era, with the euphoria of winning a war unleashing a backlash against anything that could be construed as un-American. Wilson's attorney general, A. Mitchell Palmer, became notorious for mounting raids against suspected Communist sympathizers, and thousands of arrests and deportations took place over the *ala Rand Paul "crazed mob"*

next several months, in flagrant disregard of people's civil liberties. Palmer's chief deputy was J. Edgar Hoover, then twenty-four years old. Hoover headed the Justice Department's newly created General Intelligence Division, whose sole purpose was to collect information on radicals, a designation applied even to mainstream suffragists. The newspaper headlines in New York were not sympathetic to the women. "Two Hundred Maddened Women Try to See the President," said one. "Two Hundred Women Attack the Police," declared another. "Suffragists Battle with Police: Burn Speech," blared a third.

Fearing more violent clashes if suffrage wasn't addressed soon, Democratic leaders cabled Wilson in Paris, imploring him to call a special session of Congress to pass the federal amendment. Wilson cabled back to Washington a request for the new GOP-led Congress to convene in special session on May 19, 1919. Although the House had passed the amendment the previous year, because this was a new Congress, it had to be voted on again. On May 21, the Republican-controlled House of Representatives passed the Susan B. Anthony amendment, 304 to 89; this was 42 votes more than required. Eloquent in its simplicity, the amendment states: "The right of citizens of the United States to vote shall not be denied or abridged by the United States or by any State on account of sex. Congress shall have the power to enforce this Article by appropriate legislation." Under Democratic control the previous year, the amendment had squeaked through with only a single extra vote. The resounding support from the GOP-led

House embarrassed the Democrats. In an effort to neutralize the Republican advantage, the Democratic National Committee, without waiting for the Senate to act, passed a resolution urging the states to quickly ratify the amendment so women could vote in the 1920 presidential election.

Debate began in the Senate on June 3, a stiflingly hot day. There was no suspense this time, and the suffragists had to force themselves to sit through the endless displays of oratory. New York senator James Wadsworth led the fight against suffrage. His wife was president of the National Association Opposed to Woman Suffrage, and their double-barreled advocacy made them the era's equivalent of a power couple. Still, suffrage looked inevitable, and the media were taking sides. The *New York Sun* noted that women comprised a third of New York's "standing army," a reference to the legion of female straphangers riding the subways to work and supporting public enterprise with their personal funds.

When the roll call vote was taken late on the afternoon of June 4, Wadsworth voted no, but the amendment passed by 66 to 30; this was 2 more than needed. The historic moment had finally arrived, and it could not have been more anticlimactic. This was the fifth time in a little more than a year that Maud Younger had sat in the gallery monitoring a suffrage debate. "There was no excitement," she wrote in her memoir. "The coming of the women, the waiting of the women, the expectancy of the women, was an old story. A whole year had passed in the winning of two votes. Everyone knew what the end would be now. It was all very dull."

The bad girls, the radicals, were surprisingly subdued. This was a time for quiet reflection, not fireworks, wrote Younger. "We walked slowly homeward, talking a little, silent a great deal. This was the day toward which women had been struggling for more than half a century! We were in the dawn of woman's political power in America."

8

A Vote for Mother

Catt couldn't bear to attend the debate. She stayed home rather than subject herself to another round of self-serving speeches in the sweltering heat. Mary Garrett Hay, Catt's closest friend, monitored the vote and phoned Catt with the results. "CCC danced all over the place and then settled down to THINK," Hay wrote. There was work to be done. Catt knew that this glorious moment would be a footnote to history if thirty-six states didn't ratify the amendment. She sent telegrams to all the governors urging quick ratification. Only five state legislatures were in session, and Catt pressed the governors to call special sessions rather than put off the vote. Another set of telegrams went out to the NAWSA organizers heading ratification committees in the states, giving them the green light to press ahead. That evening, a good number of congressmen and their spouses stopped at Suffrage House, the NAWSA headquarters, to offer their congratulations to Catt, who received the well-wishers with Hay, her loyal lieutenant, standing at her side. The two had been living together

since the death of Catt's husband in 1905, when Hay res-
cued Catt from the immobilizing grief and depression she
experienced after her loss. Like so many of the partnerships
formed during the fight for suffrage, the two women com-
plemented each other. Where Catt was high-minded and
statesmanlike, Hay was prickly, abrasive, and crassly political. Other women found Hay impossible to deal with, but
Catt liked her unvarnished style and was grateful for the
friendship. Their bond was unbreakable.

Congress did not set a timetable for ratification, but suffragists wanted quick action. The political outlook was
favorable and a race soon commenced among the states for
the honor of which would be first to ratify. Wisconsin,
Michigan, and Illinois were the prime contenders, and all
three ratified the amendment on June 10. Wisconsin
emerged the winner when the father of a suffragist caught
the first train to Washington and hand-delivered a certified
copy of the legislative action to the secretary of state, who
provided a signed statement that Wisconsin's ratification
was received first. Kansas was the first state to call a special
session and the first to make legislators pay their own travel
expenses to attend. As the ratification drive got under way
in 1919, fifteen of the forty-eight states had full suffrage,
with thirteen additional states permitting women to vote
in the presidential election. These so-called presidential
rights states were Catt's brainstorm. She had discovered
that it was easier to get local legislatures to approve a
change that didn't directly affect their reelection. With the
exception of New Mexico, the West was fully enfranchised;
the Midwest was checkered, and east of the Mississippi,

only Michigan and New York were in the full-suffrage col-
umn. The map looked more progressive when the presidential rights states were added, but the geographical
differences in receptivity to women's political rights
remains evident today, with women in western states running for and holding public office in greater numbers than
their eastern sisters.

Alabama was the first state to defeat ratification, with
Georgia rapidly doing the same. This was no surprise.
More troubling to Catt and the others was the lack of
momentum in the West. By the autumn of 1919, only two
western states had ratified—Montana and Utah. The ominous pause spurred Catt to hold "Wake Up America" con-
ferences in twelve states, with speakers from the Children's
Bureau and the Committee on Social Hygiene, about the
cleansing effect women would have on the body politic
once given the vote. The governor of New Mexico called a
special session after Catt's Santa Fe conference. This gentle
kick in the pants helped put several states over the top, so
that by mid-February 1920, when the NAWSA convened
in Chicago for a final victory celebration, thirty-two state
legislatures had ratified suffrage. Twenty-four of those legislatures had acted in special session, a testimony to Catt's
lobbying network. Governors typically resist special sessions because of the potential for political mischief, and the
added cost.

Wilson by then was out of the picture. Always an uncertain ally, he suffered a stroke after barnstorming across the
country by rail to promote the treaty he had negotiated at
Versailles, which included the League of Nations. Edith

took control, isolating the president from everybody but his doctors and leaving the country to guess about the gravity of his condition. From September 25, 1919, until mid-January 1920, Edith ran the government, keeping secret the true state of her husband's health. As weeks stretched into months and rumors flew, Senate Republicans openly ridiculed Wilson's "petticoat government." Wilson was awarded the Nobel Peace Prize in 1919 for his work on the Treaty of Versailles and his vision for a world organization to settle disputes. He was too sick to accept the medal and too weak politically to persuade the Senate to ratify his beloved treaty. Told he would have to compromise to win passage, he stubbornly refused any and all amendments and counseled his fellow Democrats to vote against the treaty, which the Senate defeated in March 1920.

Wilson also was powerless to do anything about prohibition, which had been ratified as the Eighteenth Amendment on January 16, 1919. Women blamed alcohol for wrecking their home lives, and its passage demonstrated the growing political clout of women even before they had won suffrage. Prohibition dried up some of the nation's excess drinking problem, but it also ushered in a criminal element. Speakeasies and rum-running gangsters flourished over the next decade in what we remember in a romanticized way as the Roaring Twenties. In 1933 the Eighteenth Amendment was repealed, relegating it to a failed experiment among humankind's efforts to improve.

·   ·   ·

As summer began, the ratification movement was stalled. Thirty-five states had voted to ratify suffrage. Only one more was needed, but the pool of likely prospects was small. The two most promising states were in New England, which had given birth to the abolitionist and women's rights movements. But Vermont and Connecticut were in the grip of conservative Republicans, and the governors refused to call special sessions. The Republican National Convention opened at the Blackstone Hotel in Chicago. The party's nominee, Ohio senator Warren G. Harding, was running on the theme of a "return to normalcy," a clever counterpoint to the ailing Wilson's failed attempt to build a League of Nations and the discomfort many voters felt over Edith Wilson's takeover of her husband's presidency. The National Woman's Party, true to its philosophy of holding the party in power responsible, picketed the convention each day with a long line of white-clad women holding banners that read: "Republicans, we are here. Where is the thirty-sixth state? Vote against the Republican Party as long as it blocks suffrage." A favorite banner carried Susan B. Anthony's admonition "No self-respecting woman should wish or work for the success of a party that ignores her sex." To placate the women, the Republicans inserted a pro-forma plank into their platform expressing "earnest hope" that the remaining Republican legislatures would act to ratify suffrage so women could vote in the election of 1920.

In contrast to earlier demonstrations, the Chicago protesters were treated more like royalty than interlopers. The police let them picket without interruption and sometimes

Women against

even helped carry their banners. On the last day of the convention, a group of suffragists went unchallenged as they draped a banner from the balcony inside the hall, where each speaker was sure to see it. It said: "Why does the Republican Party block suffrage? We do not want planks. We want the thirty-sixth state." Harding's wife, Florence, had been instrumental in her husband's victory, lobbying the five hundred male delegates, an unprecedented act of boldness for a woman at the time. She was accustomed to getting along in a man's world, having worked as an executive at the newspaper owned by her husband's family in Marion, Ohio. Harding readily agreed to meet with the suffragists once he was back in Washington, but whatever progressive ideas his wife might have had, he apparently did not share. The women found him evasive on the subject of suffrage. He wouldn't make any promises about pressuring the Republican governors of Vermont and Connecticut, and they in turn remained immovable.

Meanwhile, the antisuffragists, frantic at their string of losses, turned to the courts. They filed several lawsuits challenging ratification in individual states on technical points that had not been raised before when considering the previous eighteen amendments to the Constitution. The opponents hoped to find a sympathetic hearing, but on June 1, 1920, the U.S. Supreme Court ruled that the Constitution meant what it said, that a majority vote in three-quarters of the state legislatures is sufficient for ratification, and states can't impose additional hurdles. The ruling was fortuitous for the suffrage side because it had the unintended effect of putting Tennessee into play.

After running into a dead end with Vermont and Connecticut, precious few states were left that might put ratification over the top. Tennessee had not yet taken up suffrage because of a clause in its state constitution that said the General Assembly (Tennessee's legislature) could not act on a federal amendment until after an election had been held and a new legislature was in place. The Court ruled that ratification was a legislative act and not subject to a referendum by the voters, which a new election implied. The Court ruling cleared the way for a special session, and the ratification fight moved to Nashville.

Suffrage leaders had some trepidation about entrusting the final vote to Tennessee because of the South's entrenched antipathy to suffrage and civil rights. But Catherine Kenny, the state ratification chairperson for the Tennessee League of Women Voters, was optimistic about passage. Women had won partial suffrage the year before, "and that gives us the whip hand," she wrote in a long analysis to NAWSA headquarters in Washington. Kenny was a fixture on the state suffrage scene, and she had already established a "ratification headquarters" in the venerable Maxwell House, a favorite watering hole for politicians. Always upbeat and energetic, she was someone who threw out the first ball at Nashville's Suffrage Day baseball game and traveled the state making speeches from the back of the Tennessee Suffrage Special. The way she saw it, the immediate obstacle to ratification was Tennessee governor Albert H. Roberts, a mild-mannered former teacher who was running for reelection and terrified of taking a stand that might lose him votes. In San Francisco, where the

Democratic National Convention was getting under way, delegates demanded a special session for the good of the party, the state, and the nation. Roberts had hoped to dodge the question until after the Democratic primary in Tennessee on August 5. But when his main opponent warned that failure to hold the session would "rob Tennessee of its chance for glory," Roberts readjusted his strategy. Word reached San Francisco on the opening day of the Democratic convention that Roberts was calling a special session for August 9.

The news surged through the convention. Democrats were euphoric. If they delivered the "perfect thirty-six," millions of grateful women would vote Democratic in November. Heading the ticket was Ohio governor James M. Cox, a competent if colorless individual whose lack of charisma was offset by a dashingly handsome and charismatic New Yorker as vice president. His name was Franklin Delano Roosevelt, and he would have to wait to fulfill his party's dreams for another dozen years. Worried about retaining the White House after Wilson's failure to sell his League of Nations and the controversy over his health, Democrats saw the emerging women's vote as their salvation. The week-long convention was a paean to women, with the delegates eager to include every plank in the platform that the women wanted. When the head of the platform committee unveiled the finished product to the delegates, he said only half-jokingly, "And if there's anything else the women want, we're for it." The party named for the first time a woman as vice chairperson of the Democratic National Committee. Though eminently qualified for the position, the fact that she was from Tennessee was no accident.

An illustration of the changing times occurred when Anne Dallas Dudley rose to deliver a seconding speech. A delegate from Tennessee, Dudley was renowned for her beauty, her blue-blood lineage, and her devotion to the suffrage cause. She had put her family status on the line and braved the derision of those who labeled all suffragists "she-males." Her oratorical skills and her wit had given the fledgling Tennessee suffrage movement legitimacy. She once famously answered the argument in a debate that because only men bear arms, only men should vote, with the quip "Yes, but women bear armies." As she approached the podium in San Francisco, the band began playing a familiar popular song, "Oh, You Beautiful Doll." The delegates started singing, and soon the entire convention was belting out the pop tune.

It was a high moment, but Catt knew there were hurdles ahead. In a four-page, single-space letter to Catherine Kenny in Nashville, Catt outlined in characteristic detail what she expected from the opposition and how to counteract it. There would be voluminous literature filled with "outright lies, innuendoes and near-truths, which are more damaging than lies," she wrote. "The 'nigger question' will be put forth in ways to arouse the greatest possible prejudice." She cautioned about taking the word of male lawmakers when polling the legislature. "So many women are inclined to accept a complimentary word as a positive pledge," she said. Men were critical to this operation. Without their support, ratification would fail. She told Kenny to create a Men's Ratification Committee, "the biggest and most important men of the state, men of every political faction, representative of all classes. Do it quick before the opposition has made it impossible. Not less than 100 men, more if you can. Print all their names on your stationery . . . no matter what it costs."

Tennessee was a state proud of its reputation for "fightin' and feudin'," and its factionalism was both political and geographical. The cities were pitted against the "red handkerchief boys" from the rural areas, and tempers over the wet/dry controversy had gotten so heated that an antiprohibitionist had gunned down a candidate for governor on a street in Nashville. Where everybody lined up in the suffrage fight was unclear, and getting them lined up right would take time. On July 17—a steamy Saturday— Catt arrived by train in Nashville, carrying one small bag and thinking she would stay only a few days. Little did she suspect that it would be five weeks before she would return home to New York.

Catt's presence in the state inflamed the antisuffragists, who rallied as they never had before. No sooner had Catt stepped off the train than a telegram went out to Miss Josephine Anderson Pearson of Monteagle, Tennessee, the state president of the Tennessee Association Opposed to Woman Suffrage. "Mrs. Catt arrived. Extra session imminent. Our forces being notified to rally at once. Send orders and come immediately." Pearson was on a train that afternoon, leaving her cool home in the mountains for the sweltering city. She checked in at the Hermitage, where Catt was staying, asking for the cheapest room for herself while booking meeting rooms on the mezzanine level to serve as a headquarters. Her tiny room was so hot and sticky that sleep was impossible. She later wrote that the only way she could endure the heat was to stand under the shower, where she composed telegrams to antisuffrage leaders around the country, imploring them to come to Nashville. When they arrived, the first thing they did was move their leader to a larger and cooler room.

Pearson had a long history of antisuffrage activity. A gifted speaker and pamphleteer, she had been the dean of a small woman's college in Missouri before returning home to care for her aging parents. Her father was a Methodist minister and her mother an ardent temperance worker, whose hatred of alcohol was rivaled only by her intense opposition to woman suffrage. In a deathbed conversation, Pearson's mother had extracted a vow from her daughter that if the Susan B. Anthony amendment ever reached Tennessee, she would work against it. Now fifty-two years old, Pearson had abandoned her academic career to devote herself to antisuffrage work, taking in roomers to make ends meet.

Pearson's strategy was to portray Catt as an "outside agitator," a loaded phrase that conjured up the image of a Yankee woman threatening the southern way of life. She had stationery printed that said: Tennessee Division of the Southern Women's Rejection League for the Rejection of the Susan B. Anthony Amendment. It was quickly shortened to the Southern Women's Rejection League. Pearson blanketed the state with appeals to women asking not for money but for "active moral backing" to fight what she called three "deadly principles" embodied in the Nineteenth Amendment. The first was the surrender of state sovereignty to federal control, always an issue. The second was Negro women's suffrage, which was not welcome in the Jim Crow South. Finally, there was what Pearson termed "race equality," which invoked the specter of a wider civil rights movement. This was a battle for the hearts and minds of Southerners, and Pearson understood how to tap into their emotional vulnerabilities as they contemplated expanding the role of women.

Meanwhile, Catt was working a different angle, which relied on a careful cataloging of where each legislator stood on suffrage. It was still three weeks before the special session, so Catt urged Tennessee League of Women Voters members to go out into the communities and visit the lawmakers where they lived. Travel was hard in the summer heat, and many lived miles from any town, but by July 25 the women had collected enough signed pledges that a majority seemed attainable in both houses. The Men's Ratification Committee had gotten off to a promising start with 207 names, including former Democratic and Republican governors and a wide array of business and labor leaders.

Pearson countered with a group of her own, called the Tennessee Constitutional League for men. It was headed by a New York lawyer and included a fair number of professors from Nashville's Vanderbilt University, lots of lawyers, and enough local politicians to make Catt nervous. Her anxiety increased when the *Chattanooga Times*, an unyielding opponent of woman suffrage as was its sister publication the *New York Times,* took the editorial position that any legislator who voted for ratification during the special session would be violating his oath of office to uphold the state constitution. It was as though the U.S. Supreme Court had never ruled. The suffrage fight was playing out on the society pages as well. "Social Leaders Oppose Vote" showed leaders of the Southern Women's Rejection League arriving in Nashville fresh from victory in Louisiana, where another southern legislature had rejected ratification. "They call us the 'Home, Heaven, and Mother Crowd' in derision," one of the opponents told a reporter, which suited her fine. She didn't want to be like the suffragists, who get down into the mire of politics.

Governor Roberts announced that the special session would convene at noon on Monday, August 9. The Democratic primary was over, and he had safely won his party's nomination. The legislators began arriving over the weekend of August 7 and 8, and as they stepped off the train, women dispensing flowers rushed forward to slip a single rose into a friendly legislator's lapel. Many men accepted the gesture, and it was better than any poll. The suffrage side wore a yellow rose, while the opposition sported the American Beauty red rose. The newspapers quickly dubbed the ratification fight the "War of the Roses."

Everybody gathered at the Hermitage Hotel, Nashville's newest and finest hotel, just down the hill from the Capitol. People milled around the lobby at all hours trading information. The lawmakers were mostly "good ol' boys," small-town businessmen, and Bible-thumping fundamentalists who did not naturally lean toward giving women more rights. Lobbyists were out in force, worried that suffrage would lead to pressure to pay women more, or to laws restricting child labor. Prohibition was in effect, and Tennessee was supposed to be dry, but liquor flowed in a lobbyist-sponsored suite, and lawmakers could be heard late in the evening drunkenly singing the opposition's theme song, "Keep the Home Fires Burning."

Concerned that ratification could be slipping away, Governor Roberts set up what today would be called a war room in the state Capitol, where the suffrage side could monitor developments and calibrate strategy. Early Sunday morning, August 8, several of the governor's aides met to analyze where each of the ninety-nine House members and thirty-three senators stood on ratification. House Speaker Seth Walker had agreed to introduce the resolution and shepherd its passage. A founding member of the Men's Ratification Committee and a close ally of Governor Roberts, Walker had been a strong supporter of limited suffrage in Tennessee when it passed in 1919, saying, "It would be a crime and a shame if the women were not given this right." Walker was late for the meeting, and when he showed up midmorning, he had a bombshell to drop: Claiming a change in conviction, he said he could no longer support ratification. The assumption was that he had caved to pressure from railroad lobbyists, who were reminding lawmakers of the favors they had showered on them, including free passage.

That night, in Catt's suite at the Hermitage, suffrage leaders met to compare notes on what appeared to be an impending disaster. The Senate was safe, but support in the House was eroding. The mood was gloomy. A National Woman's Party member told of confronting Walker in the hotel lobby to demand: "What brought about your change, the Louisville & Nashville Railroad?" Walker retorted, "That's an insult!" He rushed off as onlookers stifled their laughter at his embarrassment. Catt had to smile. Though she had long disapproved of the confrontational tactics of Paul's acolytes, this was a moment she could savor. The suffragists decided to have only Tennessee women, who were more attuned to the sensibilities of southern men, lobby the legislators. Paul's radicals would take a backseat. "Graciousness is our watchword," the women agreed. Suffragists who wanted to sneak a cigarette were advised to confine that controversial activity to their hotel room.

On Friday, August 13, the fifth day of the session, after only three hours of debate, the Senate voted for ratification, sending the resolution to the House. The margin of victory was huge, with twenty-five ayes and only four nays, with two abstentions.

It was a substantial win for the suffragists and a sweet victory over the lawmakers who heckled them with verbal broadsides against "petticoat government." When one senator gleefully pointed out that this new breed of women doesn't wear petticoats anymore, a parade of suffragists formed outside the Senate chamber to lift just enough of their skirts to prove him wrong. The language inside the chamber deteriorated to the point where one senator referred to "low-neck, high-skirt suffragists who know not what it is to go down in the shade of the valley and bring forth children." At that point a woman wearing a yellow sash shouted from the gallery, "I've got six children!" Not to be discouraged, the senator concluded with a sly dig at "an old woman down here at the Hermitage Hotel, whose name is Catt—I think her husband's name is Tom—trying to dictate to Tennessee's lawmakers."

In a letter written to a friend after the Senate vote, Catt reported, "We are up to our last half of a state. . . . It is hot, muggy, nasty, and this last battle is desperate. Even if we win, we who have been here will never remember it with anything but a shudder!"

Catt thought her phone was tapped, and when she returned to her room one afternoon to find a bottle of whiskey under her pillow, she was convinced the opposition was trying to discredit her. When a friend said the libations were a gift from a friendly newspaper reporter, a woman, Catt still felt uneasy. She went on a long drive that afternoon and stashed the bottle in the crevice of a distant stone wall behind a blanket of poison ivy. Paranoia was rampant on both sides; nobody knew what Monday would bring when the House reconvened. Lobbyists wooed legislators with offers of business loans and lucrative jobs, and threatened them with loan foreclosures and political retribution. In an interview with the *Memphis Commercial Appeal*, Joe Hanover, the 30-year-old Memphis legislator who was leading the suffrage forces in the House, was asked if he feared vote-trading, a euphemism for legislators *opponents willing to play dirty*

altering their vote to satisfy some special-interest lobby. Hanover said he was prepared for that. Indeed, that very Sunday morning, an older legislator whom Hanover had befriended had knocked on his door, hung over from an evening of conviviality with lobbyists, to happily announce, "Sorry, Joe, but I'm going to have to leave you suffrage boys. The antis just paid me three hundred dollars." Hanover eyed the bleary-eyed legislator and said, "Well, you're a pretty cheap vote—I hear they're paying the others a thousand." "Why, those dirty crooks!" the farmer cried. He was back in the suffrage camp and richer for it by $300.

The legislative maneuvering held few clues to the eventual outcome. A motion to adjourn until the next morning passed on Tuesday, August 17, by fifty-two to forty-four, a margin that suggested the opposition had the votes to kill the amendment. But if they did, why hadn't they called for the vote? The threats and counterthreats got so ugly that the suffragists set up all-night patrols in the hotel and at Union Station for fear that some of their legislators might try to abscond. They couldn't afford to lose a single vote. Lawmakers got false calls about illness at home and being needed by their family. Women claiming to be suffragists were phoning Hanover's room with suggestive invitations that could put the young bachelor in a compromising position on the eve of the big vote. More troubling were calls from anonymous men who warned Hanover that his life was in danger if he didn't back off. One of only two Jews in the General Assembly, Hanover had come to America as a child with his family, fleeing from

pogroms in Poland. He was an eloquent defender of freedom, democracy, and suffrage. When Governor Roberts
heard what was happening, he assigned a Nashville police
captain to act as Hanover's bodyguard. As the suffrage
strategy meeting broke up that night, Catt said, "There is
one more thing we can do—only one. We can pray."

Knowing history would be made one way or the other,
the suffragists showed up in their marching clothes, the
white dresses with yellow sashes that had become such a
familiar spectacle over several decades. By nine-thirty, the
galleries were filled and the Capitol police directed people
outside, where they could wait on the lawn. Inside the
chamber, the suffragists had strung yellow banners
between the marble columns and attached a sunflower to
the spread eagle mounted on the wall behind the Speaker.
But as they looked down from the galleries onto the floor,
they could see red roses popping up as the lawmakers filed
in for the vote. The suffragist responsible for tracking
Harry Burn of Mouse Creek, a farm community in eastern
Tennessee known for its antisuffrage attitudes, noticed the
red in his lapel and mentally crossed him off her "hopeful"
list. Burn at twenty-four was the youngest member of the
legislature, and she had hoped he might be receptive.

There was nothing in the young man's outward manner
to suggest the turmoil he was experiencing. A letter had
arrived that morning from his mother, Mrs. J. L. Burn,
urging him to vote for ratification. Febb Emsinger Burn
had never openly identified with the suffrage movement,
but she instinctively supported voting rights for women.
As a widow who owned land like any man but still

couldn't vote, she knew firsthand what it was like to be underrepresented. Between milking cows and churning butter, she kept up with the wider world, reading four newspapers. Following the coverage of the special session, she was disappointed that her son had not come out in favor of suffrage. She understood that his constituents—her neighbors—were bombarding Harry with cards and letters stating their opposition to ratification. She decided to write him with a plea for the other side:

Dear Son: Hurrah, and vote for suffrage! Don't keep them in doubt. I notice some of the speeches against. They were bitter. I have been watching to see how you stood, but have not noticed anything yet. Don't forget to be a good boy and help Mrs. Catt put the "rat" in ratification. Your Mother.

The last was a reference to a cartoon that showed an old woman chasing the letters RAT with a broom to complete ratification. Harry Burn had no idea what he was going to do as he headed toward his desk on the House floor. He was torn between his duty to represent his constituents and a need to be true to himself and his mother's convictions. Cheers went up from the suffrage side when a prosuffrage senator who had recently had surgery unexpectedly appeared and was assisted to his desk. Tally sheets were adjusted to show that only three of the ninety-nine House members would be absent. The suffragists counted forty-seven votes on their side, two votes short of the majority needed for ratification.

It was a closing call . . .

Speaker Walker gaveled the House to order at 10:30 A.M. Dozens of lobbyists remained on the floor, making offers and counteroffers in blatant disregard of House ethics rules. The sergeant at arms hustled them to the rear of the hall, where they stood behind a railing, tally sheets in hand, ready to record each vote. After several windy speeches by lawmakers, the Speaker handed his gavel to a well-known antisuffrage member and strode confidently out onto the floor. In a legislative maneuver that signaled that he knew his side—the antisuffragists—had the votes, he proposed that the amendment "goes where it belongs—to the table." Tabling the measure would be a mercy killing as opposed to outright defeat. "Second the motion!" cried out several members. The roll call got under way. It was alphabetical, so Harry Burn's name came up early. The apple-cheeked lawmaker voted to table the amendment. Everything was unfolding just as the suffragists feared until they got to a fellow named Banks Turner. He did not answer, and after a long pause, he was listed as an abstention. The roll call continued. Turner, a Democrat, was in a state of high anxiety. He had just come from the governor's office, where he had been summoned for a last-minute telephone plea from his party's presidential nominee, Governor Cox of Ohio, about how important suffrage was to the Democratic cause in November.

Just as the final vote tally was ready to be announced at forty-eight for tabling and forty-seven against with one abstention, Turner rose to his feet. "I wish to be recorded as against the motion to table," he said.

There was pandemonium in the House. The tie vote meant that ratification was not yet dead. Speaker Walker couldn't believe it; he had been so confident. He demanded a recount, and as the clerk called out each member's name once again, Walker sat with Turner, whispering urgent entreaties into his ear, his arm draped across the recalcitrant lawmaker's shoulder to show what good buddies they were. The suffragists thought for sure that all was lost as Walker called in whatever chits he had. But when the time came for Turner to recant, he threw off Walker's arm and with a flourish in his voice shouted "Nay."

It was a tactical victory for the suffragists, but they were still one vote short of the forty-nine they needed for a majority. Walker immediately called for a vote on the amendment. No more games; he would defeat ratification outright. Once again, the roll call began. Two ayes were followed in quick succession by four nays. Harry Burn was the seventh vote, and his barely audible "Aye" went by so fast and without fanfare that it took a while for many in the chamber to realize what had happened. A low murmur spread across the galleries, but there were no overt displays of emotion, not until this third roll call of the day was complete. Anything could happen. As the roll call continued, the crowd grew quiet. Even those fanning themselves against the heat were motionless. All it would take is Banks Turner relenting to Walker, and the amendment would go down. When Turner offered a robust "Aye," Walker leaped to his feet with one last parliamentary card to play. He changed his vote to support the amendment, a move that paved the way for a motion to reconsider. It was a ploy to buy time. Only a member voting with the majority has the right to bring a motion to reconsider, but it has to be done within seventy-two hours. That meant the opposition had until noon Saturday, August 21, to overturn the fifty-to-forty-six vote for ratification.

The desperate last-minute gamesmanship did not lessen the joy the suffragists felt. They cheered; they sang; they hugged each other; they danced in the aisles. Lawmakers tossed their yellow boutonnieres into the air, and yellow rose petals fluttered through the chamber. "There were a few tears of Job but for the most part this was no time for weeping," said the *New York Times*. Conspiracy theories flourished about what favors might have won over young Harry Burn, and whether Seth Walker was a secret ratificationist because his maneuver had given the suffragists fifty votes, an unassailable constitutional majority in the ninety-nine-member House. Lawyers working for the opposition had been preparing a legal challenge against a forty-nine-vote ratification. Burn's honor was under attack. Accused of accepting a bribe and threatened with prosecution, he rose in the chamber the next day to explain his change of vote. Rejecting what he called the "veiled intimations and accusations regarding my vote," he said, "I know that a mother's advice is always safest for her boy to follow, and my mother wanted me to vote for ratification." Febb Ensminger Burn wired suffrage headquarters in

Nashville, "I stand squarely behind suffrage and request my son to stick until the end."

With the clock ticking toward the Saturday deadline for Speaker Walker's motion to reconsider, the two sides swung into action. The opposition held "Save the South" rallies all over the state to generate public protest while turning up the heat on lawmakers with a combination of threats and inducements. Nobody buckled under the pressure, but keeping the so-called "Sterling 49" in town and ready to vote was a challenge. One legislator, whose child was sick, agreed to stay for the Saturday vote only when suffrage leaders promised to charter him a train home for the princely sum of $615. Another lawmaker showed up in the House chamber recovering from a gunshot wound suffered two days earlier at a raucous party.

It was showdown time, but only nine antisuffrage legislators appeared in the House chamber that Saturday morning. The remaining thirty-eight had fled Nashville and were holed up rather publicly in the lobby of a hotel just over the state line, in Alabama. They called themselves the "Red Rose Brigade," and their goal was to deny a quorum in the Tennessee House to forestall action on the reconsidered amendment. But they were well short of the number needed to shut down the House. Business commenced instead with the "Sterling 49" firmly in charge. The House chaplain, a foe of suffrage, opened the session with a prayer that "God's richest blessings be granted to our absent ones." As soon as the clock struck noon, ending Speaker Walker's seventy-two-hour reprieve, the lawmakers voted down the motion to reconsider, and the ratified amendment was on its way to the governor's office and then to Washington. Carrie Chapman Catt boarded a train for Washington. She hoped to be present when Wilson's secretary of state, Bainbridge Colby, signed the proclamation announcing that the Nineteenth Amendment was now part of the Constitution.

Colby ordered that he be notified the moment the Tennessee certificate arrived, even if it meant waking him up. The opposition was filing all sorts of legal challenges, and he didn't want to risk further delay. Colby got the call at 3:45 A.M. on August 26, 1920, and after checking a few points with his legal adviser, he signed the proclamation without ceremony in his home. Catt's train pulled into Union Station at eight o'clock that morning. She phoned Colby's office and was told the deed was done. A *New York Times* editorial praised Colby for the understated way he brought the long struggle for suffrage to an end. Calling it an inspired diplomatic move, the *Times* noted that the absence of a signing ceremony avoided having to say which faction of the suffrage movement deserved greatest credit for the amendment.

Young Harry Burn kept a bodyguard nearby when he went home after his vote, but he was reelected to a second term in the Tennessee legislature. In an interview many years later, he said he always believed women had a right to vote. "It was a logical attitude from my standpoint. My mother was a college woman, a student of national and international affairs who took an interest in all public issues. She could not vote. Yet the tenant farmers on our farm, some of whom were illiterate, could vote. On that roll call, confronted with the fact that I was going to go on record for time and eternity on the merits of the question, I had to vote for ratification."

Epilogue

Antiwar sentiment was strong in 1920, and both presidential candidates vying to replace Woodrow Wilson saw women as a force for peace. "Mothers Will Check War," read the headline on the story reporting the candidates' reactions to the ratification of the Nineteenth Amendment. "The civilization of the world is saved. . . . The mothers of America will stay the hand of war," declared Democrat James Cox. Warren Harding and his running mate, Calvin Coolidge, made direct appeals to women, urging, "For your own good—vote Republican. Four years ago, Democrats promised to keep us out of war—four months later we were in the war."

Twenty-six million women cast votes in the 1920 presidential election, helping to elect Harding, an ineffectual and corrupt president. The hand of war was stayed for the moment, but it was a generalized sentiment and not specific to women. In the 1930s public opinion polling showed 77 percent of the people thought it was a mistake to have entered the war. Carrie Chapman Catt dedicated herself to furthering international peace. "The woman movement is safe," she said in a radio talk. "It is the one place in this troubled world where no armies are being raised and where victory is certain, but the men worry me."

Only one of the Founding Sisters present at Seneca Falls in 1848 was still alive when the Nineteenth Amendment took effect in 1920. Charlotte Woodward, ninety-one, as a teenage farm girl rode with friends to Seneca Falls to watch the proceedings from a back row and signed her name to the Declaration of Sentiments. Seventy-two years later, she was the sole survivor.

The ambivalence about women's role in society that led so many women—and men—to reject suffrage is summed up in this 1920 ode, "To a Modern Woman":

You've got the vote and you think it's your mission,
To go to the polls like a bum politician
And while you are voting, your husband must roam
For something to eat which he can't find at home.
He's getting dyspepsia and can't work for pain,
Your children neglected, ask for you in vain.
While you make speeches from a broken soap box.
Your family is wearing soiled clothes and torn socks.

Almost as soon as women got the vote, they took it for granted. It was as though the decades of struggle had never happened. They resumed their lives, caring for families and communities. Voting rates for women dropped nearly as precipitously as they did for men, a reality that Catt, who died in 1947, at age eighty-six, would find despairing. "Women have suffered an agony of soul which you can never comprehend that your daughters might inherit political freedom. That vote has been costly. Prize it," she urged.

Alice Paul, a generation younger than Catt, continued to lead the National Woman's Party. She saw the right to vote as a first step to giving women equal rights, and in 1921 she wrote an Equal Rights Amendment that was rewritten in 1943 and propelled forward in the 1970s as part of the modern women's movement. The ERA failed to pass the required number of state legislatures and fell prey to a vicious battle among women over whether it was really needed and whether it would force women into military combat and same-sex rest rooms. The amendment said simply: "Equality of rights under the law shall not be denied or abridged by the United States or any State on account of sex." The desk where Paul penned the amendment is on display at the Sewall-Belmont House on Washington's Capitol Hill, where Paul lived from 1929 to 1972. The house was and still is the headquarters for the National Woman's Party, which no longer functions as a political party and is an educational museum. A picture on the wall shows Paul in her last years in a nursing home with a quilt across her lap that says "ERA." She remained faithful to the end.

Now a National Memorial

Belmont - Paul Women's Equality National Mon. Renamed by Obama 2016

Bibliography

Andersen, Kristi. *After Suffrage: Women in Partisan and Electoral Politics before the New Deal*. Chicago: University of Chicago Press, 1996.

Baker, Jean H. *Votes for Women: The Struggle for Suffrage Revisited*. New York: Oxford University Press, 2002.

Dorr, Rheta Childe. *Susan B. Anthony: The Woman Who Changed the Mind of a Nation*. New York: Frederick A. Stokes, 1928.

Griffith, Elisabeth. *In Her Own Right: The Life of Elizabeth Cady Stanton*. New York: Oxford University Press, 1984.

Harper, Ida Husted. *Life and Work of Susan B. Anthony*. Indianapolis and Kansas City: Bowen-Merrill, 1899.

———, ed. *History of Woman Suffrage,* Vol. 6. New York: Source Book Press, 1922.

Irwin, Inez Haynes. *The Story of Alice Paul and the National Woman's Party*. Edgewater, FL: Denlinger's Publishers, 1977.

Jacobs, William Jay. *Mother, Aunt Susan, and Me: The First Fight for Women's Rights*. New York: Coward, McCann, & Geoghegan, 1979.

Johnston, Johanna. *Mrs. Satan: The Scandalous Saga of Victoria Woodhull*. New York: Popular Library, 1967.

Kraditor, Aileen S. *The Ideas of the Woman Suffrage Movement: 1890–1920*. New York: W. W. Norton, 1981.

Lemons, J. Stanley. *The Woman Citizen: Social Feminism in the 1920s*. Champaign: University of Illinois Press, 1973.

Marshall, Susan E. *Splintered Sisterhood: Gender and Class in the Campaign against Woman Suffrage*. Madison: University of Wisconsin Press, 1997.

Papachristou, Judith. *Women Together: A History in Documents of the Women's Movement in the United States*. New York: Alfred A. Knopf, 1976.

Roberts, John II. *Rating the First Ladies: The Women Who Influence the Presidency*. New York: Citadel Press, 2003.

Sochen, June. *Herstory: A Woman's View of American History*. New York: Alfred, 1974.

Stanton, Elizabeth Cady; Susan B. Anthony; and Matilda Joslyn Gage. *History of Woman Suffrage. Vol. 1, 1848–1861*. Rochester, NY, London, Paris: Source Book Press, 1899.

Stern, Madeleine B. *Purple Passage: The Life of Mrs. Frank Leslie*. Norman: University of Oklahoma Press, 1953.

Stevens, Doris. *Jailed for Freedom*. Troutdale, OR: New Sage Press, 1995.

Van Voris, Jacqueline. *Carrie Chapman Catt: A Public Life*. New York: The Feminist Press at the City University of New York, 1996.

Ward, Geoffrey C., and Ken Burns. *Not for Ourselves Alone: The Story of Elizabeth Cady Stanton and Susan B. Anthony*. New York: Alfred A. Knopf, 1999.

Weatherford, Doris. *A History of the American Suffragist Movement*. Santa Barbara, Calif.: ABC-CLIO, 1998.

Winner, Julia Hull. *Belva A. Lockwood*. Niagara Falls, NY: Niagara County Historical Society, 1969.

Woloch, Nancy. *Women and the American Experience*, 3rd ed. New York: McGraw-Hill, 1999.

Yellin, Carol Lynn, and Janann Sherman. *The Perfect 36: Tennessee Delivers Woman Suffrage*. Oak Ridge, TN: Iris Press, 1998.

9 781684 422272